PRAISE FOR S
THE SCIENCE O

I love this book! Michael Fullar
with new and creative ways to approach the challenge of educating students in the current period by showing how spirit work and collaboration can advance learning and increase support for students. Timely, thought provoking, and inspiring, *Spirit Work and the Science of Collaboration* will be a tremendous resource for educators searching for ways to make education more meaningful and transformative in the years ahead.

—Pedro Noguera, Dean
Rossier School of Education, University of Southern California
Los Angeles, CA

Our current social and political climate is rife with distrust, suspicion, cynicism, and tension. Michael Fullan and Mark Edwards provide important insights into how schools can navigate these contemporary challenges. *Spirit Work and the Science of Collaboration* offers much more than tips and practical advice; it provides us with a healthy reminder that such an undertaking necessitates reflection, persistence, love, courage, and the audacity to envision new possibilities for collaboration in schools.

—Gerardo R. López, PhD
Professor, Michigan State University
Editor-in-Chief, *Educational Administration Quarterly*
Past-President, University Council
for Educational Administration

Michael Fullan and Mark Edwards have penned a must-read for all educators. They demonstrate the power of collaboration regardless of where a district is in the country, its size, or its demographics. Schools do not just improve; positive change does not just occur. The real work required to transform education, preserve democracy, and ensure the survival of our planet is going to take a lot of deeply committed people collaborating, seeking solutions, and finding answers. *Spirit Work and the Science of Collaboration* is a fantastic guide for that task.

—Terry Grier, Retired Superintendent
Houston Independent School District
Educational Leadership Consultant
Wilmington, NC

We live in complex times. That is certainly not a new statement, but what we hopefully have learned is that there is not a better time to move forward in a better way, where we are more inclusive and thoughtful in our actions. In *Spirit Work and the Science of Collaboration,* Michael Fullan and Mark Edwards do not just inspire us to want to go deeper with our practices and be more human in our interactions—they use real examples to help show us how to do it.

—Peter DeWitt, EdD
Leadership Coach, Author, *Education Week* Blogger
Moderator of *A Seat at the Table*

Spirit Work and the Science of Collaboration captures the essence of what school leaders need to make learning more transformational for students and to make our relationships more inspiring and fulfilling. Michael Fullan and Mark Edwards tap into how to operationalize spirit and collaboration by giving examples that get results from eight exemplary superintendents from diverse systems across the United States. Read, discuss, and apply this practical and universal wisdom.

—Patrick Sweeney, Leadership Coach
Retired Superintendent, Napa Valley Unified School District, CA

True to what we have come to expect, the authors raise a new concept, spirit work, within constructs with which we are familiar—relationships, trust, collaboration, well-being, and pedagogy. Delving into the science of collaboration and sharing illuminating examples gives deeper meaning to the old proverb, "If you want to go fast, go alone; if you want to go far, go together." *Spirit Work and the Science of Collaboration* offers direction and hope in a time when it is badly needed.

—Laura Schwalm, Retired Superintendent
Garden Grove Unified School District, CA
Chief of Staff, California Education Partners

Buckle up for a moving and instigating read. Michael Fullan and Mark Edwards present major global and social threats to our very existence as humans. Their solution? The unqualified need to provide every student with the true, right, and just education currently enjoyed by only some. We learn from and with actual school districts audacious enough to invoke the power of the human spirit and collaboration as drivers of radical change in education. Through these real-life examples, we are fortified by what we desperately need at this moment in history—learned hopefulness.

—Robin Avelar La Salle, Founder and CEO
Orenda Education Sierra Madre, CA

By connecting these two new phenomena of spirit work and collaboration, Michael Fullan and Mark Edwards present educators with what they describe as a revolutionary potential for future learning, highlighting ways in which spirit work can be a force that drives not only self but collaborative efforts for change in school districts. *Spirit Work and the Science of Collaboration* introduces an alternative to traditional ways of thinking about system change and expands our ideas of learning and transformation.

—Ann E. Lopez, Professor, Teaching
Department of Leadership, Higher and Adult Education
Director, Centre for Leadership and Diversity
Ontario Institute for Studies in Education
University of Toronto
Co-Editor-In-Chief, *Journal of School Leadership*
Toronto, Ontario, Canada

The authors make a compelling case for why both spirit work and collaboration are important elements for transforming learning in significant ways. This book is uniquely written, using real examples to describe the behaviors of leaders that result in the conditions that foster both elements.

—William Hite, Superintendent
The School District of Philadelphia, PA

It's never been more important to learn from leaders who lead by example and from their heart, soul, and spirit. The eight models of spirit work and collaborative science captured by Michael Fullan and Mark Edwards represent some of the best and brightest thinking in school system leadership. As the nation works diligently to navigate through the COVID environment, enacting change that best suits the unique circumstances in every school community is essential in today's public education landscape.

—Daniel A. Domenech, Executive Director
AASA, The School Superintendents Association

Spirit Work and the Science of Collaboration

My admiration and thanks to
the myriad leading practitioners whom I learn from.

—Michael Fullan

In honor of my parents, Dr. Bill and Ernestine Edwards,
two lifelong educators who did spirit work
every day of their lives.

—Mark Edwards

Spirit Work and the Science of Collaboration

Michael Fullan

Mark Edwards

Foreword by Margaret J. Wheatley

A JOINT PUBLICATION

FOR INFORMATION:

Corwin
A SAGE Company
2455 Teller Road
Thousand Oaks, California 91320
(800) 233-9936
www.corwin.com

SAGE Publications Ltd.
1 Oliver's Yard
55 City Road
London EC1Y 1SP
United Kingdom

SAGE Publications India Pvt. Ltd.
B 1/I 1 Mohan Cooperative Industrial Area
Mathura Road, New Delhi 110 044
India

SAGE Publications Asia-Pacific Pte. Ltd.
18 Cross Street #10-10/11/12
China Square Central
Singapore 048423

Printed in Canada

Library of Congress Control Number: 2021944645

ISBN 978-1-0718-4549-3

This book is printed on acid-free paper.

President: Mike Soules
Associate Vice President and Editorial Director: Monica Eckman
Senior Acquisitions Editor: Ariel Curry
Senior Content Development Editor: Desirée A. Bartlett
Senior Editorial Assistant: Caroline Timmings
Production Editor: Melanie Birdsall
Typesetter: Hurix Digital
Proofreader: Theresa Kay
Cover Designer: Scott Van Atta
Marketing Manager: Sharon Pendergast

21 22 23 24 25 10 9 8 7 6 5 4 3 2 1

CONTENTS

FOREWORD

To Be Fully Human

Margaret J. Wheatley

This exceptional work offers us a pedagogy, a philosophy, a petition, a plea for how to be fully human and how to awaken the richness of our human spirits in our classrooms and educational systems. Skillfully placed in the context of our time, relying on decades of experience, illuminated by compassion and clear seeing, this is a book you must put into practice. And the good news is you already have experienced what the authors are describing. Let me prove this by asking you a few questions:

1. Recall an experience of true collaboration, a time when you felt part of a group that worked well together and created good solutions.
2. Now think about how the group worked together. What went on between members of the group? What was the level of interplay, exchange, honesty, humor? What about leadership?
3. How did you feel as you participated in the group's process? How did you feel afterward, even now, as you remember that experience?

Experiences of true collaboration are always identical, no matter your age or cultural background. We feel connected, energized, empowered, inspired, creative, and purposeful. We don't get lost in ego needs or power plays. Together, we just want to get the work done, the problem solved. Looking back on these experiences, we recall the joy we felt at being together, giving it our best, persevering. Even when we didn't succeed, or our accomplishments were short-lived, these moments of collaboration and communion still fill us with satisfaction, even joy.

We need to remember and trust these experiences more than ever as this world descends into conflict and polarization, as we struggle to work together with colleagues, as meetings erupt in anger and fear, as social media entitles hate-filled anonymity. In neuroscience terms, our brains are functioning to ensure our survival; with so much threat, we can only behave like animals. In evolutionary terms, we are devolving, forgoing millions of years of evolution that lifted us beyond the animal realm, the evolution that blessed us with cognition and consciousness—and community.

This is where we are now, but the wisdom of how to be fully human—to exercise our great human qualities of generosity, compassion, creativity, caring—this wisdom is still alive in all who have experienced true collaboration. With humility, let us note that our modern-day experiences validate what Indigenous cultures have known for tens of thousands of years. Even though these cultures have been devastated by Western societies' intention to destroy them, their wisdom is still present. I spent many years working in South African communities that lived the spirit of *Ubuntu*—a person is only a person through other people. I exist through you, and you exist through us. When I asked a young man what "Ubuntu" meant, he was puzzled by my ignorance, and then quietly said, "It means being human."

From Indigenous peoples, from migrant communities, from impoverished communities, from communities suffering from natural disasters, I've learned this truth: Humans can get through anything as long as we're together. Whatever the problem, community is the answer.

For teaching purposes, Michael Fullan and Mark Edwards have described collaboration and spirit work as two separate dynamics, but in my experience (and hopefully in yours), these two dynamics weave together like a Mobius strip of infinite possibilities and discoveries. Collaboration is not a process or technique. It is a means to discover what it feels like to be fully human, to experience the human spirit. Whatever the collaborative process, it is only when we connect at a deeper level—when we let go of our individual needs and focus on what the work needs from us—only then do we experience breakthroughs, insights, and possibilities beyond our expectations. Something palpable has changed, something new has entered the room. My explanation for this experience is in the Bible: "Whenever two or more are gathered, there will I be also." (The Quakers note that a meeting feels gathered when there is "a sense of the meeting.")

This is our work, to be the carriers of this knowing, to rely on our experiences of collaboration to give us the confidence and courage to be champions for collaboration in our schools and communities. But where do we find the motivation, the energy to resist succumbing to fear and anger, to not be overwhelmed by despair, to stay awake and persevere?

We find the answer when we recognize that in all that we do as educators, parents, community members, our work is to recognize, value, defend, and protect the human spirit. Especially now—when life is under siege, when decisions are made that destroy human and planetary futures, when policies are designed to drive us apart, to push us into survival mode so we can be controlled by fear—now is the moment when we must step forward as champions for the human spirit. This is true spirit work, and we will accomplish this by turning to one another, consciously choosing to collaborate, and persevering amid increasing setbacks and pushbacks. This is not the work of cowards. It is the work of pioneers.

Like all pioneers, like the leaders featured here, we are willing to venture forth to discover places of possibility because the old ways are too destructive, because we can no longer tolerate staying where we are. If we stay here, our spirits will shrivel, life will lose meaning—we will survive but perish. So, we set out. We have no idea of the trials and tribulations that await us. We only know we have to leave; we have to try. As we journey forward, the path demands that we keep letting go. We make progress only by letting go of what holds us to the past. Because we must abandon so much, we learn what we must never let go of, what is of true value, what we must protect no matter what. With this clarity, fueled by our faith in the human spirit, we continue.

At the end of our journey, may we find contentment in noting:

> We were together. I forget the rest.

Margaret J. Wheatley, EdD, began caring about the world's peoples in 1966, as a Peace Corps volunteer in post-war Korea. In many roles—speaker, teacher, consultant, advisor, formal leader—she acts from the unshakeable conviction that leaders must learn how to invoke people's inherent generosity, creativity, and need for community. As this world tears us apart, sane leadership on behalf of the human spirit is the only way forward. Since 1973, Meg has taught, consulted, and advised an unusually broad variety of organizations on all continents (except Antarctica). Her clients and audiences range from the head of the U.S. Army to twelve-year-old Girl Scouts, from CEOs and government ministers to small-town ministers, from large universities to rural aboriginal villages. She has served as full-time graduate management faculty at two universities and has been a formal advisor for leadership programs in England, Croatia, Denmark, Australia, and the United States. Through Berkana, she has advised leadership initiatives in India, Senegal, Brazil, Zimbabwe, South Africa, Mexico, Greece, Canada, and Europe.

Meg received her doctorate in Organizational Behavior from Harvard University, and her master's in media ecology with Neil Postman from New York University. She studied at University College London and the University of Rochester for her bachelor's degree.

She has authored ten books, from the classic *Leadership and the New Science* (1992; in 19 languages) to *Who Do We Choose to Be: Facing Reality, Claiming Leadership, Restoring Sanity* (2017). Her new work is a CD + book, *The Warrior's Songline*, a journey into warriorship guided by voice and sound. Since 2015, she's been training leaders and activists from 35 countries as Warriors for the Human Spirit. This is the work of the rest of her life.

Her websites are designed as rich libraries of materials for those seeking to lead and organize in life-affirming ways: www.margaretwheatley.com and www.berkana.org.

PREFACE

In his classic *Structure of Scientific Revolutions* (1962), Thomas Kuhn argued that "paradigm shifts" (alterations in the principles that govern models of thinking and action) occur under two conditions, both of which are essential. One requirement is that the current model is patently no longer working—indeed, Kuhn used the phrase "catastrophically failing." Such a situation might result in chaos and massive destruction and even extinction, but it will not contain the seeds of progress to a better system solution. For the latter, says Kuhn, you need a viable, reasonably worked out alternative. The problem is that it is hard to develop the new paradigm while the old system exists. What you need are some pioneers who not only know that something is wrong but also perceive early lines of fruitful new development and take the risks to test and push it into further action until the examples begin to be noticed by others, who then become second-order change agents joining in to further the development and depth of the new model and its spread.

In this book, we have identified eight school districts in the United States that represent elements of new learning in action on a system (districtwide) basis. This work is especially heroic these days, where we're under conditions of extremely negative physical disasters (climate change) and social forces (inequality and plummeting mistrust and associated anxiety and declining mental health). These cumulative and mutually reinforcing negative forces threaten our very existence.

Up until very recently—let's say until the arrival of the deadly COVID-19 virus—disaster reality seemed isolated and/or distant. Then, a torrent of negative phenomena seemed to happen at once, daily and ubiquitous, leaving most people reeling. A strong foreboding feeling is now upon us.

In the past, most of us—if we thought about it all—reckoned that the future would work out. It always did. Now there are palpable doubts, and they are rising. In this book, we draw on two powerful phenomena that animate human life and have the potential of reversing the current negative trends. They are *spirit work* and the *science of collaboration.* We will investigate the meaning and nature of these two concepts, how they play out in action, and with what consequences in eight districts across the United States. We will wonder about the implications for transforming learning across many other districts. The good news is that there is a growing realization and hunger to act, especially among the young. The problematic news, back to Kuhn, is that there are many forces that hold even bad systems together. We think that a positive future for learning and schools resides in the increased spirit work and the associated science of collaboration. We offer these eight case examples of what such development looks like and entails in its early stages. And we believe that the ideas could become part and parcel of a new wave of transformation and learning in society.

This is the second time that we (Michael Fullan and Mark Edwards) have come together having arrived at similar conclusions—one through practice-based academia, the other through deep practice. For a decade (1994–2004), Edwards had been a pioneer in advancing one-to-one computers in Henrico County Public Schools, Virginia. He then moved to become superintendent at Mooresville Graded School District (MGSD), where he was superintendent from 2007 to 2016. As Edwards moved deeper into quality implementation, his intuitive and experienced sense of the problem and solution drew him to Fullan's books on the culture of organizations—notably, *The Six Secrets of Change* (2011a) and *Leading in a Culture of Change* (2020a).

Fullan's books both reinforced and extended what Edwards was learning. These compatible ideas were then captured in a joint book, *The Power of Unstoppable Momentum* (2017). We documented how embedded the new ideas were in MGSD. Educators from across the United States were flocking to attend the summer courses and professional learning that permeated MGSD culture. The core factors at work consisted of an interrelated synergy among *a culture of learning, engaging pedagogy, continuous assessment and feedback, a human resource pipeline of learners and leaders, and a commitment to identifying and sharing lessons learned that could be shared widely.*

In 2017, we went our separate ways. It has turned out that the context for education reform has dramatically changed over the past five years. As we show in Chapter 1, society has worsened, and traditional education has become less and less fit for our complex times. At best, only about a quarter of students see a sense of purpose, in relation to life, for the education they are experiencing. COVID-19 has exposed these problems dramatically, but they were there prior to the pandemic.

COVID-19 has caused many things, and perhaps it was the stimulus for us to get together again. Whatever the case, we connected again in 2021 and compared notes. We quickly discovered that we had remarkably similar notions about what was happening and, more significantly, what some people were seeking by way of solution—not just district leaders, but also some students, teachers, parents, and communities.

While the overall situation is grim, there are educators and students who are seeking and, to a small extent, finding new ways forward. These action-oriented modern pioneers are not superhuman individuals, but those with a deep sense of human purpose, indeed, human evolution. As we seek and study these groups, we sense that they are moving beyond moral purpose to what we call "spirit work." The word "spirit" has many origins, but it can be understood through the Latin *spiritus*. It means "breathe life into." It is associated with the soul—the essence of what it means to be fully human, the caring of ourselves, others, and the universe. Somehow, under the conditions of climatological threat and social fissure, learning can take on a new, more fundamental meaning. Love and caring become animated as some leaders see deeper and more fundamental challenges and aspirations linked to a better and necessary future. Such are the eight leaders and many others in the districts we examine.

The second fundamental concept and, indeed, partner to spirit work, is the science of collaboration. As Meg Wheatley observes in the foreword, good collaboration is "what it feels like to be fully human, to experience the human spirit." By this, we don't mean the ordinary idea of working together. New developments in neuroscience make collaboration a powerful phenomenon in the evolution of humanity. We will delve into these exciting and new phenomena to show how spirit and collaboration represent the revolutionary potential for the future of learning. Our leaders see collaboration not as a means to an end, but as something deeply human. Whether you find the source of working together in incredibly complex times in a god or religion or in the neuroscience of evolution, it is different. There are many fissures and deep conflicts across the globe and within countries and neighborhoods. But there are also many examples of people working together to solve deep problems. We believe that the human spirit has a tendency to join with others to solve the deepest problems (we will see it in the eight case examples). More broadly, human spirit offers a source of hope for the future—what we call *learned hopefulness*. Learning has a giant role to play at this juncture in our evolution.

We believe that the human spirit has a tendency to join with others to solve the deepest problems.

But let's face it: in both physical and social domains, the good side is losing, and it is losing in real time. Are the districts we feature the dying gasps of a good breed, or are they Lazarus-like figures that signal that good life might re-assert itself? It could go either way, but we are optimists and good at reading the tea leaves, and we believe that the 2020s can be a time of transformation that reverses the current disaster-infused trends.

We think then that there are nascent elements of this new future for learning that are beginning to appear. We have identified eight districts across the United States that demonstrate aspects of spirit and collaboration indicative of the trend that we sense is at an inchoate stage. We don't claim that they are the best examples in the country (let alone the world), but we do say that there are many others like them out there—not superhuman but driving ahead despite major barriers. They are on the right track, even though early in the journey. Their leaders don't think that the obstacles they confront are bad luck, but rather problems to be solved on the way to a new future. We will find ideas in these cases that point the way to that future.

We do not consider these cases as representing the only way to the future of learning. We present these cases not as pure exemplars, but rather as illustrations of promising pathways and progress therein despite the odds. We hope they will give courage to other schools and districts making or wishing to make similar inroads to the future. Subsequent chapters provide case studies of the districts grouped according to small, medium, and large size. We hope that these cases will serve as pioneers at the very early stages of what might become a very new order of public schools devoted to the future of society. Let's be explicit: modern learning exemplified through the young may be our only chance. Fortunately, we have many people who are willing to go down that path where spirit and collaboration join forces.

PART I

THE CHALLENGE OF THE CENTURY

Transforming Learning

1 THE PROSPECTS FOR RADICAL CHANGE

There are three major reasons why a new purpose for public education is needed. One is that the world is rapidly deteriorating and needs citizens with greater capacities and a sense of civic duty. The second is that the current system is not serving the needs of the majority of students. The third is that new knowledge, skills, and ideas are now available for what powerful learning should look like.

RAPIDLY DECLINING GLOBAL TRENDS

Much of the evidence on the first point has been summarized in Fullan and Gallagher's *The Devil Is in the Details* (2020, Chapter 1) and Fullan's *The Right Drivers for Whole System Success* (2021). There are four interlocking and mutually reinforcing negative trends that are now causing a rapid downturn in the prospects for our planet surviving in the next 50 years. We list them in Figure 1.1 with nicknames (unflattering as they are).

Wallace-Wells, in *The Uninhabitable Earth* (2019), documents in excruciating detail how just about all aspects of the earth's ecosystem are decaying in a mutually interacting death spiral (heat, hunger, water, wildfire, oceans, unbreathable air, plagues, climate—you name it; all going bad). Inequality has been in a downward fall for at least the last 40 years. New analysis by a new breed of economists (mostly women, as it turns out) documents in detail how the lion's share of gross domestic product (GDP) goes to the top narrow percent of owners and shareholders, while the wages of middle and lower

1.1 Global Trends 2021+

1	2	3	4
Climate Collapse *(disintegrating)*	Inequality *(galloping)*	Social Trust *(plummeting)*	Mental Health *(staggering)*

classes have barely moved over the four decades (Boushey, 2019; Mazucatto, 2018). Social mobility (the idea of doing better than your parents) has stagnated since the late 1970s (see Fullan, 2021). Social trust is plummeting. Putnam and Garrett's (2020) sweeping and well-documented trends in the United States since the 1870s show clearly that trends of "I-ness" (self-centeredness) have become increasingly strong since late 1970. Among other negative effects, perceptions of social trust declined from 58% in 1960 to 33% in 2010 (and, we would speculate, even lower in 2021). Numerous surveys—local and global, of all ages, including the very young, rich, and poor—show increasingly greater anxiety, stress, and ill health (all of this before COVID-19).

Each of the four elements in Figure 1.1 causes the other three to worsen, thereby intensifying and greatly accelerating the trends.

SCHOOLING

When it comes to fundamentals, schooling hasn't changed much in the past 200 years. The basic "grammar of schooling," as it is sometimes called, has remained essentially the same over the years. These characteristics include

- An approach to teaching as the transmission of existing knowledge (teacher to student).
- A system of batching of students by age, grade, and subject.
- Egg-crate classrooms led by individual teachers.

- Uniform scheduling.
- Testing by grade and/or subject coupled with accountability.
- An ignoring or miscasting of the inequity problem.
- Custodial and sorting roles of schools.
- Separation of parents/communities from schools. (Fullan, 2020b)

In a recent issue of the *American Journal of Education*, guest editors Jal Mehta and Amanda Datnow put out a call for research papers that focused on the "long-lasting and core elements of schooling" (2020). Five papers were eventually approved for publication. The editors asked Larry Cuban of Stanford and Michael Fullan to comment on the papers. What we found in the published papers was a collection of partial and basically in-vain attempts to alter how schooling was experienced by students. All four of us as commentators drew the same conclusion: there was little that was new in terms of providing engaging and meaningful learning for students as they face a new and complex world (Fullan, 2020b). This is less a criticism of schools as it is a recognition of a deeply entrenched system.

The consequences for students (and teachers) are monumental. Various surveys and studies show that a greater and greater percentage of students either tune out or mechanically do the work to get the grades. Heather Malin, Director of Research at Stanford University, conclused after several studies that only about 24% of senior high school students (i.e., those who were succeeding in the system) "have identified and are pursuing a purpose for life" (Malin, 2018, p. 1). Various other studies have found mounting disengagement as students go through the grades, as well as increased anxiety across socioeconomic status groups.

Mehta and Datnow characterized the state of affairs as the "yawning gap" between how schools are organized and how youth learn. They describe five attributes that youth need for positive development:

- Strong connections to adults and peers
- To be viewed in asset-based ways
- For their identities to be valued
- The opportunity to contribute to the world
- Opportunities to do work that has purpose and meaning (Mehta & Datnow, 2020, p. 492)

What is clear is that there is a major mismatch between what students need and what many of them want and how schools are organized and function. It has become a crisis for learning and for society.

In a recent report, *The Right Drivers for Whole System Success*, Fullan (2021) documents how academic obsession and the accompanying narrow curriculum have alienated the majority of students including what one researcher called "the wounded winners"—those who were technically successful but stressed out and/or doing things that had little interest for them.

Fullan also showed how social intelligence (the equivalent of the science of collaboration) was poorly developed—a point to which we return in Chapter 3. No matter how you cut it, existing schooling does not serve or interest the majority of students, nor of course their teachers. Aligning the daily work and experience in schools with what students need to be ready for their future requires significant change. Students need to understand what is relevant to their futures and their needs as human beings, and they are innately connected to the vital need of changing how we teach and how we learn. Last, the future no longer seems like it is distant. It increasingly feels like the present and the future are happening on the same day!

COVID-19 entered this bleak picture in early 2020 and, in a word, has discombobulated the world everywhere and in every way. The Fullan and Quinn Deep Learning team completed an assessment that it released in June 2020, *Education Reimagined* (Fullan et al., 2020). Sticking with our theme that education is in need of big change, note that COVID-19 has exposed numerous flaws in the current system, including access to technology and opportunity to learn, along with creating enormous strain on virtually everyone and every aspect of learning. It has also got people thinking: *Could we take the opportunity to alter learning? Can students play a more active role in shaping their own learning? Can parents and communities become more active partners with schools? Now that standardized tests have been suspended, can we take the occasion to replace them with better alternatives? As well-being has become an essential priority, could we move to balance or integrate well-being and learning? One thing seems certain: schooling will never be the same, but how should the new system be fashioned?* These questions favor the themes in this book: a chance to transform learning in a significant way, a chance to identify and foster spirit work and the science of collaboration.

The idea is not just to survive COVID-19, but to end up much better than was the case, for example, in 2019. Our book takes on new meaning because of the crossroads at which we find ourselves. The challenges are so enormous that it would be easy to slip into familiar paths of routine learning: more technology, hybrid learning with students as passive learners, large-scale commercial learning, schooling as custodial places for the young, and so on.

Or we could take the opportunity to significantly revamp learning and schools. The cases we present—with their foundational components of spirit and collaboration—could be early examples of what might be needed to leverage the pandemic experience into transformational change. We also know that schools and districts that had strong spirit and focused collaborative cultures did much better in dealing with the disruption. A small-scale example of this phenomenon can be found in the work that Fullan does with Michelle Pinchot, a school principal in Garden Grove Unified School District in Anaheim, California. In the first instance, Fullan linked with Pinchot when she was moving from one principalship to another—a school called Heritage Elementary—in Garden Grove in 2017. The proposition was whether a principal who had developed a highly successful collaborative school (a version of our science of collaboration) could also do so in another school that had low degrees of joint work. The answer is a resounding *yes*, which we documented in our article "The Fast Track to Sustainable Turnaround" (Fullan & Pinchot, 2018).

With COVID-19 we faced a new question: Could a strong collaborative school not only withstand but even thrive in the face of the onslaught of a deeply disruptive pandemic? Again, the answer is a strong affirmative. Immediately upon the shutdown in March 2020, the school launched into collective action as follows:

1. Working in teams remotely: the school created socio-emotional learning lessons, daily schedules, identified student needs (academic/social), developed interventions, formulated remote expectations, established collaboration schedules, had check in-checkout (CICO) systems for at-risk students, organized mentoring and student recognition systems, and created tech support and tech collaborations.
2. Working in teams to support virtual learning: organizing home visits, books, materials, food distributions, troubleshooting technical problems, and having back-up counseling.
3. Meeting twice a week to reinforce a single focus, celebrate success, set goals, review student needs, stay connected and continue to grow current leadership teams, monitor progress, reflect, and re-design. (Pinchot & Fullan, 2021)

The lesson here is that strong collaborative organizations are better equipped to confront crises, and indeed to thrive in them (we called our article "Testing Sustainability"). By contrast, individualistic cultures are not equipped to respond to threat (or, for that matter, to seek out innovations). Of course, in Heritage, we are only talking about one school, while in this book we are examining hundreds of schools in eight different districts. But the principle is the same: the science of collaboration is a generative capacity.

> Strong collaborative organizations are better equipped to confront crises—and indeed to thrive in them.

INNOVATION AND NEW IDEAS

We might say then that our third reason why a deeper purpose for education could be in the cards is what we call "the taste of change." In complex, chaotic times, organizations that rise to the occasion paradoxically become even more ambitious than they were pre-crisis. The new themes of spirit and collaboration are inspiring some schools and districts to be dramatically more proactive relative to the immediate future. Recall Kuhn and his scientific revolutions in which he noted that unequivocal failure is not sufficient to unseat the existing model. The positive examples we studied have additional significance as possible ideas for a new future—ideas that could help unseat the old outdated model of schooling.

Thus, we need examples of new models that contain the elements and themes of success. Both of us, in separate work over the past five years, have begun to notice and, in some cases, enable exceptions to the negative trends. Fullan and the team found promising new trends around 2014 when they began a partnership with clusters of schools in different countries around the theme of "New Pedagogies for Deep Learning" (Fullan et al., 2020; Quinn et al., 2020). This deep learning focused on global competencies rather than standard tests, on new learning designs distinct from the old grammar of schooling, and on changes in the culture of collaboration within and across the infrastructure of schools, districts, and the center (policies and structure).

Parallel to Fullan's experience, Edwards began to see districts that were on a different trajectory. Despite the barriers (or maybe because of them, in a rise-to-the-occasion sense), these districts were on the move when they should have been faltering. As we connected with the idea of producing this book, we found greater impetus from the experiences in the pandemic—a now-or-never commitment to go deep and go long.

It seems, then, an ideal time to pull together these emerging ideas to build better education systems. New factors—some negative, some positive—have become evident. Here are eight themes that are more prominent in the past 18 months:

1. Well-being
2. Parents and community
3. Technology
4. Innovation
5. Leadership or lack of leadership
6. Deadly inequality
7. Students as agents of learning and change
8. System transformation

Together, they provide the seeds of transformation.

As a list, they are not strong enough to unseat the existing paradigm. The four faces of global implosion (climate collapse, gross inequality, reeling social distrust, and deteriorating mental health) as a set represent a powerful negative reason to take action. Similarly, but less directly, widespread dissatisfaction with schools represents another source of pushing for better futures. Then the more positive lighthouse trends of new possibilities that we document in this book become a welcome part of the mix.

CONCLUSION

We can now turn to examine in more depth the two prominent new trends that we see emerging in school districts that are attempting to break through to new possibilities—spirit work and the science of collaboration. In some ways, it is a mystery as to why and how they would emerge at this particular time. In a real sense, we see this as part of evolution. When things become complex, when dire problems erupt and spread, and when consciousness and subconscious evolve, chances are that new ways of thinking and feeling emerge and, as such, become cultivated through the complexities of our fascinating humanity. In another way, who cares how new trends come about? The fact is that we may have new opportunities to reverse the course of our recent bad history and to revitalize learning as a force for improving our future. Finally, as we shall show, if you have a sense of the new neuroscience of learning, you will know that a greater sense of spirit will generate a propensity for deeper collaboration and vice versa. Spirt and collaboration become fused. This is the human odyssey that Meg Wheatley writes about. Are we able to accomplish radical change in learning in this decade? On a large scale, we feel that the prospects are touch and go. Read this book with an eye and a heart to what you can do individually and together to work with young people and others to usher in, barge in, or whatever it takes, to change learning, thereby changing society.

Time to start the journey!

2 SPIRIT WORK

Spirit work may sound like an odd phrase at first. Why not be content with *moral purpose* or *moral imperative*—titles of Fullan's earlier books? Moral imperative is something to be embraced; where does spirit take us? Spirit, as we said in the preface, extends and is part and parcel of being human. In another sense, it seems larger than life, but it is more like humans at their evolutionary best. If we take a simple notion of who humans are, we can include *genes* (how we have changed and adapted to the universe in ways that affect who we become biologically without our knowledge), *culture* (ways of acting and relating that the group values), and *consciousness* (what we say we believe and know). Only one of these, the latter, is part of our knowing self (Campero, 2019). The other two are subconscious. We will see in this chapter how our evolution and who we have become is largely beyond our deliberate control, has occurred without our consent, has increasingly taken on a supernatural status, and is still something that we want to claim as human. The more we delve into spirit work, the more we want to improve ourselves and others, even though we might not fully understand it. What we see happening in spirit work is the emergence of leaders who believe that individuals and groups either have no limits or are not close to reaching them. In education, this means that leaders love their students in a way that potentially becomes an open-ended concept. This is the line of thought we take in these next two chapters, and into the subsequent three chapters with the eight districts. Let's go back a bit earlier.

In October 2003, Dalton McGuinty (and his Liberal Party) was elected as Premier of the Province of Ontario. The previous party, the Conservatives, had been in power for eight years.

As of 2003, high school graduation in its 900 secondary schools was stuck at 68%; literacy and numeracy (using Ontario's high standard) were mired at about 55% for Year 3 and Year 6 in the province's 4,000 elementary schools. One of us (Fullan) was appointed as McGuinty's Chief Policy Advisor. We immediately set three goals:

1. Raise the bar substantially in literacy, numeracy, and secondary school graduation.
2. Close the gap between high and low performers (with respect to socioeconomic status and considering English language learners [ELLs] and special education students).
3. Increase the public's confidence in the public education system (where 95% of all students attended).

This is not the place to examine the strategies used (see Fullan, 2010), but let's consider the results: steadily and over the next decade, scores increased substantially in literacy, unevenly in math, and significantly in high school graduation. Relative to the latter, the percentage of secondary school graduates (the 900 schools) climbed from 68% (2004–2005) to 86% (2016–2017). Put another way, there were over 200,000 students who would not have succeeded had the rate of graduation remained at its 2003 level. Moreover, the gap between ELL students and those born in Canada was almost eliminated after three or four years as a very large group of new immigrants arrived.

These accomplishments were impressive and exciting, but they were not spirit work in action. Instead, it was good strong moral purpose for what we called "raising the bar and closing the gap for all students regardless of background." It was suitable to the first decade of the 21st century (and, to a certain extent, still is; see Fullan, 2010). Much has changed in the decade since, mostly for the worse: climate deterioration threatens the planet, inequality gaps have galloped with the top 10% scooping the lion's share of financial gains at the expense of the middle and working classes, anxiety and mental illness at all ages have climbed, social trust has plummeted, the majority of students in secondary schools find little purpose in schooling, and even the seemingly successful (graduates) are not well off.

As we concluded earlier, COVID-19 and the accompanying pandemic have made matters worse in the short run, but it also exposed deep problems already in existence. The larger agenda is to transform the public education system over the next decade. But what can we make of the existing system? Despite horrendous and ever-worsening conditions, some school districts are bucking the trend. Indeed, they are succeeding *because* of the very challenges they are facing. It is here where we find spirit work evident—a powerful concept that we can admire under the current system, and leverage on a large scale for the future.

In summary, what we did in Ontario in the first decade of the 21st century was impressive but was carried out under conditions that were far less challenging and less complex than is the case twenty years later. We call the new developments *spirit work* because the leaders in question, as well as the others within the eight systems examined, seem to rise to the occasion. The questions become *What did they do that was so special, and why and what are the implications for the next phase of reform (the 2020s)?* We will return to these matters in the final chapter.

SPIRIT WORK

Spirit is the essence of character—what it means to be human. We will contend that new seemingly larger-than-life actions are essentially extending the boundaries of what it means to be human. It is the valuing and love of all things that are alive. It is the desire for oneself and others to thrive and prosper in ever-complex situations. It is embracing how we relate to and help others be the best versions of themselves.

In our deep learning work, we define progress as helping people to live effectively in the increasingly complex universe of the 21st century. More specifically, we define flourishing as a "process of becoming and the outcome of being" with respect to purpose, identity, belonging, contribution (to others and the word), and self-efficacy (Fullan, Quinn, & McEachen, 2018). More directly, for this book we define *spirit work* as the actions and accomplishments that leaders and members of school districts undertake to help their members cope and develop under the complex and adverse conditions of contemporary society. Put bluntly, it is what leaders do when they value spirit but are facing massive odds and obstacles in the course of their daily work. Spirit work is how we characterize the core attributes and work of the leaders and other members of the eight districts featured in Chapters 4, 5, and 6.

We define *spirit work* as the actions and accomplishments that leaders and members of school districts undertake to help their members cope and develop under the complex and adverse conditions of contemporary society.

We have been true believers about the ultimate importance of culture and relationships as key drivers for student and teacher success for many years. The advent of the pandemic, social justice issues, and numerous other related challenges has spurred deep thinking about what is needed for public education to survive, evolve, and ultimately thrive. We have seen significant indications that we should focus on two main foundational elements to build upon. The first we refer to as *spirit work*—we believe that understanding how culture, relationships, and shared beliefs interweave with productivity and happiness is essential for students and teachers to thrive. Connecting daily work with the understanding of how creating a spirit force field undergirds all efforts will propel individuals and teams to learn and grow together. Developing spirit in schools and school systems means that everyone is respected and counted on to be an integral contributor to creating, maintaining, and growing the spirit. Students need to know and believe that they can be part of creating a better place by sharing and creating spirit that can lift, sustain, enrich, and energize teaching and learning.

If you will allow one meta-comment from evolutionary biologist E. O. Wilson in *The Origins of Creativity:*

> Science owns the warrant to explore everything deemed factual and possible, but the humanities borne aloft by both past and fantasy have the power of everything not only possible but conceivable. (2017, p. 70)

Wilson is saying that science has limits (which indeed are expansive), but the human mind does not have any logical limits. What was once superhuman is no longer thought to be (such as spirit work where virtually *all children* learn how to thrive in a super complex universe).

In the rest of this chapter, we indicate various elements of spirit in order to give a sense of its dimensions in action, which we flesh out later in the case examples.

SPIRIT CONSTRUCTION

No school or school district just happens to have high levels of spirit work in action. We believe that it's not just about cognizance and working on spirit elements, but about creating the flow of daily life that includes and reinforces the elements of strong spirit: trust, faith, hope, conversations, happiness, and love. Students, teachers, and all school employees can contribute to the spirit and benefit from the lift, of being part of a family of spirit learners. It's like everyone is building this force field that gives everyone a big lift the minute they walk in the door. Students, teachers, administrators, and parents will testify to the very real effect this force field of spirit can have. They all say the same thing: "You can feel it!" By sharing in the construction of ubiquitous spirit, everyone shares the responsibility and the benefits at the same time. Doing this work together, through conversations and daily endeavors, creates a fuel of synergy and mutual forward motion. Shared purpose, connecting people to their work together, for, and with each other, is a powerful force.

TRUST

It takes time to build trust when everyone is needed and vital to creating it. How do you build trust? Consistency is at the heart of trust. Teachers and students must know that every day they work in a caring, loving, and supportive environment and that they are responsible for creating their mutual trust. Respect for others and embracing shared responsibility for trust-building is central to this element. Students and teachers don't just go to school; it's where they live a lot of their lives. Students spend half their lives in schools, and living in a place where people are connected and feel appreciated is important beyond words.

Working through tough stuff is a sure way of building trust. When students and teachers know that if they are struggling, someone will be there to help them get through it, it lights the flame of endurance. Students who understand that they are not just recipients, but are architects of learning, become leaders for each other. Teachers need to trust that principals are consistent in their leadership. Trust dies with inconsistency and a failure to provide support for students and teachers to get through tough times.

CONVERSATION

It makes sense for everyone to understand and to be a part of what's going on, but it is important to know that it takes effort to build coherence. Students and teachers need to engage in constant dialogue about what they are doing and how they are doing. Learning how to lead and inculcate productive conversations with students and with each other is essential work for teachers. Principals who are in constant dialogue with teachers and students about the work they are doing are creating coherence through conversations. Students learn from instructional conversations with each other and not just the curriculum of the content area, but the curriculum of life. Conversations light the path of learning together and lead everyone to a broader insight into a problem or how to solve the problem. Learning to listen together creates connections for learning and growing with each other. Listening to each other is a loud message of respect. One of the most vital skills for student readiness in life is to be conversant. Having the confidence and the capacity to engage and work well with others requires daily practice and experience in talking and listening together.

FAITH

Trust can lead to faith, and parents want badly to trust and have faith in their children's schools. Students want and need to have faith in their teachers, and teachers need to have faith in their principal. When students hear teachers tell them "I have faith in you," it is hugely important. Every great teacher we have ever known understands how to establish trust and faith with students. Being fair, consistent, thoughtful, and supportive are daily messages that, over time, can translate to faith. Great faculties build on trust to create faith in each other. Teachers who show daily kindness, persistent expectations, major patience, and converse with students establish foundational faith in the value of the organization.

CONVICTIONS

We have observed teachers who have deep convictions about each student. This goes beyond commitment to a deeper and firmer sense of belief. Over the years, we have seen teachers and faculties that demonstrate what we would call "extreme efficacy" for each student. Students feel it and know when their teachers have that kind of conviction for them. We're-in-this-together dispositions provide assurance and vital emotional support. When a new teacher joins a faculty and is met with big spirit collegiality, they become part of the shared conviction—part of a force field for success.

LOVE

Children learn better in a loving environment. Teachers teach better in a loving environment. Everyone who works in a school system works better in a loving environment. Over the years, we have heard teachers say, "I love our students" and you can see in the eyes of the students how important that statement is. Affirmation of each other, and of each other together, creates a gentle breeze of comfort and well-being that does immeasurable good.

LAUGHTER AND HUMOR

Children need to laugh and want to laugh, and they love laughing together. If you find a school with students who are happy, you are likely to find more learning going on. Students need to see their teachers smile. This is big stuff. Real big!

LIGHT AND HOPE

Spirit is a force field that creates the light for the path ahead and gives hope to students and teachers. Spirit work creates the conditions and the relationships that maximize learning and growing. We need each other more than ever before. We need everybody's creativity and caring and open hearts to find our way through. We can help one another by trusting. A hopeful future is possible. As we take up in the next chapter, on the science of collaboration, we can't get there alone—we can't get there without each other.

What we are saying is that the 21st century commenced with some difficult problems in the development of the basics (for example, in literacy, numeracy, high school graduation). Second, we observe that the situation has become rapidly much more complex and compounded by other new developments (climate change, social and economic deterioration, the pandemic) that have radically and increasingly changed *the context* for schooling—making it much more complex, which in turn is feeding on itself to become ever more challenging. The districts that we have identified, on the one hand, can be thought of as being caught in the middle yet still rose to the occasion, so to speak. Further, these districts may contain lessons that enable us to consider implications for the next phase of education, which we do in the final chapter.

CONCLUSION

We are not able to explore the full human potential of spirit-embedded living in this book. We are extremely grateful that Dr. Margaret Wheatley has developed some of these connections in the foreword. We would all do well to learn from and with First Nations and Indigenous cultures. We believe and hope that this will be the next phase of human development.

We will see in the eight case examples in this book that learning and caring are based on deep spirit and loving. Everyone counts; the leaders in our cases have a transcendent stance when it comes to negative environments. Despite more than 20 years of a system that crushed many a sense of spirit through a narrow curriculum, and a regime of narrow testing, the districts and the leaders we feature in this book, against huge odds, *made spirit prevail.* It seems that spirit leaders can transcend negative environments (and eventually could be part of a movement to spread it more widely). Our case examples show the depth and power of spirit in the human condition: you can suppress it, but you cannot keep it down.

A core part of new spirit work is *well-being for all.* Well-being should have been a core part of learning all along, but in modern times it has given way to academic learning. As the latter gained prominence (and ironically, we would say) there has been the rise of ill-being—stress and anxiety among students, parents, and teachers. Fullan (2021) documents in detail how academic obsession has dehumanized learning to the detriment of learning itself and of well-being (the wounded winners who pay the price through deteriorating mental health).

Spirit work helps to restore and establish grander scenarios. One of Fullan's team members, Dr. Jean Clinton, is a child psychiatrist and neuroscientist at McMaster University just west of Toronto (the kids call her "Dr. Jean"). As we got closer to our work on deep learning and the global competencies (the 6 Cs that we will talk about later), we asked Dr. Jean to define what it means to become "good at life" (our way of getting at *well-being*). Here is her response:

> People become good at life when they feel safe and valued and have a sense of purpose and meaning. There is a need to be engaged in meaningful activities that contribute to the well-being of others. In the face of adversity, being able to navigate to the resources that you need to get out of the situation—known as *resilience*—is an essential component. To get there, one needs to identify values, goals, and needs as well as personal strengths. The competencies you need to achieve these, I think, are the 6Cs [character, citizenship, collaboration, communication, creativity, and critical thinking] as long as compassion and empathy are emphasized. (personal communication, 2020)

This is spirit work in action: helping to get all young people ready for an increasingly complex world. In Chapter 3, we revisit Dr. Jean and neuroscience to learn more about the science of collaboration, the complementary twin of spirit work. Once we explain and underpin system change with spirit and collaboration, we will examine the dynamics of real change in the eight districts in the three chapters of Part II.

3 THE SCIENCE OF COLLABORATION

We might have just as well have said the *neuroscience* of collaboration. Brain research, as it is sometimes called, has been uncovering the knowledge that humans are born to connect, that with more and more of the right kind of connection, the capacity of the brain becomes great and greater—more neural pathways, greater short-term and long-term memories, more insights, more creativity, and much more. *There is no theoretical limit to what humans can do individually and collectively.* This is not just because they are learning more, but mainly because their capacity to learn and create is expanding.

There is no theoretical limit to what humans can do individually and collectively.

But given the way things are happening in the world these days, things can go wrong, so let's start with a lesson from evolutionary biology that Mary Jean Gallagher and I described in our book, *The Devil Is in the Details* (Fullan & Gallagher, 2020). The argument is complex but not difficult to amass and understand:

1. Humans do not have a special place in the universe: we lucked out due to evolutionary developments that ended up privileging us with big brains and capacity therein.
2. Humans are not automatically intrinsically good. Each of us is conflicted; sometimes we are selfish, and other times

we commit to the common good. We (our team) believe that goodness has the edge, but it needs certain conditions to prevail.

3. Our evolved brains are born (neurologically) to connect: we communicate, recognize, bond, cooperate, and compete "from all these the deep warm pleasure of belonging to our own special group" (Wilson, 2014, p. 75). *But* this can easily go wrong; depending on our (especially) early experiences, we can find ourselves isolated in our own inbred group, or alone in the world.

4. D. S. Wilson (not related to E. O.) states: "Modern evolutionary theory tells us that good *can* prevail, but only when special conditions are met. That's why we must become wise managers of evolutionary processes. Otherwise, education takes us where we don't want to go." (Wilson, 2019, pp. 13–14)

5. "This means that an evolving population is not just a population of individuals, but also a population of groups." (Wilson, 2019, p. 77)

The reader does not have to believe in the evolutionary track to grasp the main point. Humans, individually and collectively, are probably inclined to connect for the good of individuals (themselves included) and for groups, *but it is not guaranteed.* Our book, in effect, says it is no accident that these eight districts have gravitated to spirit work and related deep collaboration. It is *natural*, not to say automatic; such outcomes must be cultivated.

As we mentioned at the close of Chapter 2, Fullan works with a neuroscientist and child psychiatrist, Dr. Jean. Fullan asked Dr. Jean whether humans have an innate propensity to connect with other humans. She said, "Absolutely!" and sent us a video that showed a man carrying an armload of books trying to open a cupboard door. A toddler was in the room with his mother on the far side of the room and happened to glance over at the man. The toddler then walked over to the man, reached out, opened the door, and walked back to his mother without any fanfare. Brian Christian (2020) commented on the same research: "Human infants as young as 18 months old will reliably identify a fellow human facing a problem, will identify the human's goal and the obstacle in the way, and will spontaneously help if they can, even if their help is not requested, and even if the adult doesn't so much as make eye contact with them, and even when they expect (and receive) no reward for doing so" (p. 251). The original researchers (Warneken and Tomasello) note that such helping behavior is "extremely rare evolutionarily" (when compared to other species; quoted in Christian, 2020, p. 252). As Tomasello puts it, "the crucial difference between human cognition and other species is the ability to participate with others in collaborative activities with shared goals and intentions" (Christian, 2020, p. 252).

Humans are born to collaborate, but then socialization occurs, whereby they may become isolated, get locked in with a given group, or flourish in cooperative endeavors with others. Out of this comes the power of the group, for better or worse. In this chapter, we will set out what "good" collaboration looks like, but first, a reminder about the connection to Chapter 2. Spirit work is also natural to humans, especially as they interact and evolve. But spirit without connection to wider groups becomes a cult or a random array of cults. It fails to be generative and regenerative in the absence of diverse human interaction. It fails to grow and consolidate in the absence of purposeful and creative collaboration. We need both the intimacy of home groups and the reaching out and inclusivity of wider connection with individuals and other groups. It requires ever-expanding connected autonomy.

It behooves us to comment on an aspect of life that most humans have neglected. Except for Indigenous peoples, the propensity for concern and connection has not applied to Mother Nature and the Universe. The latter, to most of us, are not considered living things. This fact alone could be the end of us. Again, from the evolutionists: "Humans have arrogantly become self-appointed and god-like rulers of the universe. We have become the mind of the planet and perhaps our corner of the universe. We can do with Earth what we please. At our peril, we chatter constantly about destroying the planet—through nuclear war and climate change" (Wilson, 2014, p. 176). As we become more aware of the depth of spirit and collaboration in the districts exemplified in this book, it is perhaps a short and natural journey to encompass all life on the planet and the universe—an invitation so profoundly articulated by Meg Wheatley in her foreword to our book, and in her lifetime of integrating spiritual and human evolution.

It is only when the two forces—spirit and collaboration—feed on each other that they can grow (or, put another way, they grow in tandem).

To sum up: in times of chaos and related disturbance, humans become anxious, combative, worried about the future. Some are drawn to higher values—what we call *spirit work*. Some leaders—the eight featured in this book—inevitably rise to the occasion. If such a rise is to become significant (whither on the vine, or expand and deepen) it must connect with (in fact, leaders must deliberatively cultivate) the science of collaboration. It is only when the two forces—spirit and collaboration—feed on each other that they can grow (or, put another way, they grow in tandem). This is what is happening in the districts we feature. They are exceptions, but in the extreme conditions we now face, they can be harbingers of what could come on a larger scale. This is by no means guaranteed, but our point—this whole book—is that the need is extreme; positive, potential deep responses (based on spirit and collaboration) are inevitable on some scale, and, in turn, the question becomes whether (and how) these instances could become in this decade potential pathways that could lead to system transformation.

THE GROWTH OF COLLABORATION

In one sense, when you look closely at any human endeavor you find that effective collaboration is at the heart of any significant success (of course, a case could be made that evil can also be served by strong collaboration, but we are hitching it to spirit). In his massive study of *The Innovators,* Walter Isaacson documents that the digital revolution was a function of good and myriad forms of collaboration where people learned from each other. Isaacson shows that the ability to work as teams time and again "made them [innovators] even more *creative*" (2014, p. 1, italics in original). Education, one would think, would have a natural advantage when it comes to learning—after all, universal learning is its stated goal. Ironically, that has turned out not to be the case. We are not going to try to get to the source of this issue, but one suspects that the controlling, batching, and sorting function of original mass schooling in the late 1800s in the United States was the main reason—a pattern that scholars call the "grammar of schooling." The historical grammar of schooling leaves little room for what we are calling the *science of collaboration.* We have already referred to Mehta and Fine's (2019) and Mehta and Datnow's (2020) research in search of deep learning, in which they found that despite claims to the contrary, focused collaboration for better learning failed to develop.

Over the years, we have had images of teaching as *the world's most lonely profession, behind the classroom door, busy kitchens,* and other signs that learning together on a continuous basis is at a premium. Despite this persistent backdrop, there have been celebrated examples of collaborative cultures in some schools and in a few district cultures. Indeed, both of us have been part of developing such schools or districts and/or studying them. In the next section, we are going to give an account of the main characteristics of such collaborative schools with the conclusion that they have been successful to a point, but do not represent either widespread or sustainable change. If we may venture a forecast, our main thesis in this book is that it will take both spirit work and the science of collaboration to complete the transformation, and even at that, it won't be successful unless this direction is picked up and prioritized at the policy level. In short, spirit without collaboration does not travel far, and collaboration without spirit represents an empty promise.

COLLABORATIVE CULTURES

Let's start back in time and build the case for better collaboration. We mentioned that deliberate collaboration in schools began at least some 60 years ago (and earlier if we think of the one-room schoolhouse, team teaching, and the like). One excellent overview of the past 30 years has been furnished by our close colleague, Andy Hargreaves (2019): "Teacher Collaboration: Thirty Years of Research on Its Nature, Forms, Limitations, and Effects." Andy takes us back to Dan Lortie's (1975) classic study of teaching in which he characterized teaching in terms of three interacting elements: *presentism* (focusing on the here and now), *conservatism* (small-scale changes), and *individualism* (working in isolation). Few chances for collaboration under those conditions one could readily conclude.

As we encountered failed implementation through the late 1960s and throughout the 1970s, one could readily see that Lortie's culture was not fertile ground for collective improvement. When Fullan began his career as a freshly minted sociologist in 1968, he was handed a career theme on a platter (one that generated five editions of *The Meaning of Educational Change* from 1980 to 2016). Among a handful of factors, failed implementation was largely caused because teachers were not working together. More serious, and the cause of the cause, was that innovations were generated without much teacher input, thereby entering Lortie's world without much to offer. Seymour Sarason observed in *The Culture of the School and the Problem of Change* (1972) that with the new math "teachers became aware of two things: innovation was in the air, and they were not in on it."

At the same time, Neal Gross and colleagues (1972) studied up close what they called an "organizational innovation" involving special education to help disadvantaged children. They found what we now call a *non-event*: nothing much happened because teachers were not clear about what to do, lacked capacity, had limited materials, and so forth. There started (50 years ago) a movement to fix implementation. Out of this came a general agreement that the effectiveness of an innovation probably depended on the quality of collaboration. As they say, "the devil is in the details." Hargreaves provides an excellent review of how collaboration was all over the map in the aforementioned (2019) article: it included *contrived collegiality,* where administration formed teachers in groups and expected them to work together; or *balkanized cultures,* where subgroups of teachers worked independently without (or against) other teachers. Professional learning communities (PLCs) came on the scene. Developed by Rick DuFour, Becky DuFour, and Bob Eaker, PLCs came to have a major presence in the United States from the mid-1990s to 2010, and to some extent still exist. One interesting finding occurred when the Boston Consulting Group, funded by the Gates Foundation, was asked to assess the nature and value of teacher learning. Teachers agreed overwhelmingly and supported collaboration, but ironically, administrators liked PLCs more than teachers did (Boston Consulting Group, 2014)! In other words, teachers endorsed collaboration, but not the PLC variety.

In the past decade, we have begun to see stronger versions of collaboration, which are beginning to identify how teachers can work more effectively. If we can be self-serving—just in time for the science of collaboration to flourish—it started for us when Hargreaves and Fullan wrote a book called *Professional Capital* (2012). We used the metaphor of capital to make the point that in teaching (as elsewhere), if you want a return, you have to make an investment. Given the history of collaboration over the past 60 years, that investment has been absent or wrong-headed; instead, we argued, we need to invest in *professional capital,* which has three components (the following is adapted from Hargreaves, 2019):

- *Human capital* is about the quality of individuals (their competence, knowledge, qualifications, and commitment).
- *Social capital,* which for Hargreaves and Fullan is the most critical one, relates to the capital that teachers have generated together through their networks of learning, strength of mutual support, shared professional development, and firm foundations of trust.
- *Decisional capital,* or decision-making, was about teachers' professional development and how it developed through experience, professional learning, mentoring, and coaching over time.

Our point here is that we are at a juncture where we can pull together the key ideas from professional capital (or, if you like, professional learning) and link it in a two-way mutual relationship with spirit work. We will pursue these twin themes in the eight cases in Part II (Chapters 4, 5, and 6) and in the overall lessons learned that we formulate in Chapter 7.

In the meantime, we don't think it is an evolutionary accident that the quality of collaboration has noticeably improved in the past five years. We see stronger and more specifically documented cases, but still very much in the minority. We highlight only a few here so that the reader gets a sense of the specific nature of these cultures. Viviane Robinson et al. (2008) conducted a worldwide review of research on the impact of school leadership on student engagement and learning. The researchers found only one factor of significance: what they called "leading teacher learning and development" with an effect size of 0.84 (generally, effect sizes of 0.40 or so are considered "weak, but statistically significant"). We have worked with this finding and generally think of it as "school leaders who 'participate as learners' with teachers in moving the school forward."

John Hattie et al. (2021) evolved his Visible Learning® work from studying the effect sizes of individual teacher practices to examining what he called "collective efficacy" (teachers in teams). With over 400 measures (e.g., student feedback, assessment, parent involvement), Hattie et al.'s findings are typically in the 0.29–0.64 range, which is relatively weak in terms of impact. However, when Hattie and team turned to measure what they called "collective efficacy," the effect size jumped to a whopping 1.27—higher by far than any of their other measures (Hattie et al., 2021, p. 21). Hattie's group identified the constellation of factors associated with great efficacy as shared belief and high expectations, evidence of impact, collaboration to identify and use high-yield teaching strategies, and the degree to which the principal participated in frequent, specific collaborations—all aspects of the science of collaboration.

In the same vein, Amanda Datnow and Muriel Spark's (2019) case studies of high-poverty-high-performing schools in California found that the day-to-day culture made the difference, specifically in terms of focused collaboration within the school day; specific, supportive norms; striving for specific evidence-based practices; buffering from external distractions; and a revealing cluster that they called "supporting teachers emotionally." Also compatible is Hargreaves and O'Connor's (2018) international research on *collaborative professionalism*, which they summarize as "the joint work embedded in the culture and life of the school."

All of this is good work, and there is more like it. The problems are that we don't know how widespread it is (5%? 10%? more?) in schools; much of it is *intra-school* research, and there are a few district-level studies that show collaborative, successful districtwide cultures—but again we don't know how widespread these are (one would suspect not so). Finally, networks of schools working together have had a long but not prominent history, and indeed are beginning to show a resurgence as individual schools or districts are proving inadequate for system reform. Some of these developments are in Europe, the United Kingdom, Asia, Latin America, Australia, and New Zealand. These worldwide examples are beyond the scope of our book, which focuses on cases in the United States. (But we would argue that our twin concepts of spirit and science of collaboration have widespread applicability.)

THE PROMISE OF COLLABORATION

From a historical perspective, our argument makes the following case. From its origin as teaching as a lonely profession, collaboration since the 1960s has made halting progress. Some good, collaborative school cultures were established over the decades, but they were limited in three ways: they (1) were in the minority, (2) were mostly intra-school, with a smattering of school districts, and (3) did not become an established part of a new culture. Over the past decade, we have begun to see examples of networks of schools, but these too did not represent system change. Recently (mostly in the past five years) there is a new and powerful surge in collaboration arising from the combination of two forces. One is the growing evidence that traditional school systems have been seen as ineffective for the majority of students and have lost their sense of purpose. The second is that the pandemic has exposed the weakness of the school system and serendipitously increased the interest in innovation and system reform as we enter the post-pandemic period. We see these developments emerging (and, indeed, we are part of networks ourselves working on this very agenda). We predict that this recent trend will take off in the current decade. By so doing, collaboration and whole-system success, including equity for all, could make major advances in the current decade.

One of us (Edwards) asked a fifth-grade student to define collaboration, and he replied, "It is doing stuff together, kinda like learning together, figuring out stuff, and building projects together." We believe that as more and more students and educators study the life of "doing stuff together, figuring out and building things together," we may have figured out some important stuff about teaching and learning. For years we have talked about collaboration as a strategy or a type of activity that may enhance learning, but if we look deeper with a scientific lens, we may very well find hidden keys to learning how doing stuff together can become a big deal. This means finding out how to best learn together. Think of the metaphor of an orchestra and how the sound created happens. Working in small groups, practicing learning together, solo practicing, putting parts together, listening together, modulating the sound—these are all part of this artistic science of doing stuff together. We believe this type of learning design is much better suited for optimizing teaching and learning and matches up what students want and need. Through the years, a lot of the collaborative effort has been a superficial and short-lived dynamic without much success. Doing complex things together takes a lot of practice and persistence to develop the skills and understanding of how to make it work. Collaboration is organic and the life of it requires continued sustenance of deliberation, reflection, and perseverance. Students want to do stuff that is relevant to them and learning together and figuring out stuff together bridges the view from the classroom to each student's future. It's about life. Creating schools where students engage in conversations and are nurtured through learning to become conversant are the kind of places where students learn best.

> Collaboration is organic and the life of it requires continued sustenance of deliberation, reflection, and perseverance.

Looking at the microsystems within the collaborative classrooms ecosystem and at the significance of doing work together and learning how to work together is exciting. Students need to talk and need to learn to engage in productive conversations. When the ecosystem supports this, they connect this to their lives. Conversation is like a nutrient to learning and propels more learning. Truly connecting with others gives us joy. The circumstances that create the connection don't matter. Inculcating personal and team cognizance that the learning environment is created and evolving by everyone every day is a powerful drive for learning and productivity. The organic culture of collaboration creates vital connections to content with the lives of students and teachers. Spontaneous discovery brings learning to life, and then students become explorers and scientists of knowledge.

Teachers need the same connective ecosystem to thrive and grow. Being a conductor of collaborative enterprise requires formative scientific observation and reflection. Instructional and productivity cueing are a focal part of the leadership role of teachers in collaborative classrooms. Collegial nurturance is as vital to adult learners and as necessary for the life of learning as it is for students. The power of knowing that you are not alone, that you are a part of the leadership equation, and that your voice matters and is necessary is profound. Fullan and Gallagher (2020) concluded that deep sustainable change across a school system happens when staff at all levels experience leading learning together. Organic collaborative professional ecosystems rely on some of the same cultural nutrients that students respond to. Formative conversations with peers and mutual nurturance with principals and others are leading the way by modeling consistent and meaningful engagements. Being part of the architecture for learning and a leader of learning is validating and motivational.

One of the most remarkable examples of collaboration that we have observed concerns Mooresville High School Senior Projects presentations in 2016. Students in the Exceptional Learning, Special Education department (students with special learning needs) were presenting to an audience of parents, teachers, and each other. One young man got up to give his presentation, which included slides. Each slide had a sentence to describe the project. This young man had interned as a custodian at a nearby university and shared photos of his work experience. The young man was ready to start when he nodded to another young man, who then got up and stood beside him. The young man who stood up then placed his hand on his friend's shoulder throughout the brief presentation. The collaborative touch enabled a student to do a presentation that otherwise would have been impossible. Everyone understood the powerful work they had just witnessed and why the ecosystem worked. In a small but critical way, we witnessed the science of collaboration joined with spirit work.

More broadly, collaboration is seen as more and more valuable. The Organisation for Economic Co-operation and Development (OECD)'s 2018 Teaching and Learning International Survey (TALIS) of teachers across many countries makes many references to the value of collaboration among teachers. Recent work from Victoria, Australia, extends the nature of social intelligence in a report, *Unleashing the Power of the Collective* (Singhania et al., 2020)—a study of 50 schools serving disadvantaged schools in networks called "the Connection." Evaluation data show gains in student engagement, student learning and development, STEM (science, technology, engineering, and mathematics)-related learning, student voice, metacognition, and general capabilities. A further example from the same group extends the application of social intelligence to potential system change (Bentley & Singhania, 2020). In addition to finding that focused networks accomplished more, the authors also uncovered that they paid more attention to "alignment with system priorities and engagement with a diverse range of actors" (p. 7). Incidentally, the latter is what we call an "increase in systemness" (Fullan, 2021).

We will see the science of collaboration, exemplified in many ways by our districts—and especially when coupled with spirit work as pointing to radical new possibilities for *system change itself*. Fullan (2021) identified this possibility in his use of the similar term *social intelligence*. Collaboration is an intelligence. When it becomes a science—based on the proven principles of the three dimensions of professional capital, and most of all when it becomes infused with spirit work—collaboration may achieve its long-sought place in promoting quality learning and quality living.

CONCLUSION

In these first three chapters, we have been setting up the argument within which we are about to examine eight districts that we think exemplify the direction that learning should pursue in depth and systematically. We badly need a transformed public school system with a new, more prominent societal role—indeed, a role in which learning helps create and lead future societies.

In the meantime, we detect a stealthy killer, namely the deterioration of social trust. Until recently, over the centuries the perception of social trust—as simple as asking "To what extent do you trust other people (in your country, the world)?"—has steadily increased (although we do not have good measures going back for more than a couple of centuries). Not so today; trust is no longer on the rise. We earlier referenced *Upswing* by sociologist Robert Putnam and his co-author Shaylyn Garrett (2020), which used qualitative thematic data to trace key societal trends in the United States from the 1890s to the present. The authors captured several periods that reflected what they called "I-ness" (self-centered) or "We-ness" (concern for others). It was not as linear as you might predict. The last We-ness period occurred before and after World War II, until the late 1970s. Since 1980, there has been a relentless and ever-deepening trend toward excessive I-ness. Recall that in the 1960s, 58% of the people reported "high social trust" in society; by 2010, social trust had "collapsed" (Putnam & Garrett's word) to 33%. We suspect that it is even lower currently, a decade later. This indicator, and others like it, are time-bombs for planet survival.

Over the past 60 years, education has become a passive recipient of a bad society. If you look closely, our book and the eight districts are, in effect, part of a movement to alter this direction. We believe that public education can and must reverse its role in order to become an active agent for establishing a new future that helps reverse the trends. Neither spirit work nor the science of collaboration individually could make a big difference. Together they might have a huge impact because they bring out and multiply the best in each other. If we are right, there are hordes of people, especially but not confined to the young, who are ready for new, deeper, sustained action. Many of these people can be found in the school districts featured in Part II.

PART II

EARLY SIGNALS

Districts in Action

THE DISTRICT CASES

Part II contains three chapters that focus on eight district cases that exemplify spirit work and the science of collaboration in action. These cases represent various types of leaders (by ethnicity, age, gender), numbers of students, and geographies. In addition to diversity, the criteria we used to select the cases included external recognition through awards and our personal knowledge of the district, their work, and their reputations within and external to the districts.

Chapter 4 focuses on three medium-size districts near the U.S. East Coast: Ithaca City School District (New York), Virginia Beach, and Rowan-Salisbury (North Carolina).

Chapter 5 examines two very large south central districts: Shelby (Memphis, Tennessee) and Jefferson County (Louisville, Kentucky).

Chapter 6 shifts to the West Coast with San Ramon Valley Unified (California), Highline (Washington State), and Chula Vista Elementary (California).

4 EAST COAST DISTRICTS (UNITED STATES) IN ACTION

ITHACA CITY SCHOOL DISTRICT (NEW YORK)

ALL YOU NEED IS LOVE

. . . and he went back to meet the fox. "Goodbye," he said. "Goodbye," said the fox. "And now here is my secret, a very simple secret: It is only with the heart that one can see rightly; what is essential is invisible to the eye." "What is essential is invisible to the eye," the little prince repeated, so that he would be sure to remember.

—*The Little Prince* (Saint-Exupery, 1943)

Each of our eight cases represents a major press forward in learning for all students under current conditions, and as such captures what can be accomplished through deep leadership. The foundation idea for Ithaca City School District is that one "sees rightly" only with the heart. In education reform, nice-sounding phrases are plentiful. The key question is: *How do powerful ideas come alive in day-to-day practice?* In Ithaca, you would not have to tell students or teachers what the fox meant by explaining that you can only see rightly with the heart. Dr. Luvelle Brown, the superintendent since 2011, has spread the word about the importance of leading with your heart. He believes deeply that every student needs to know that they are loved and cared for. He has been leading learning in this small

Dr. Luvelle Brown

but complex district for a decade and has been relentlessly consistent in insisting and imploring all staff to teach with love and care. His constant smile and warm affect have set the tone for leaders, teachers, and students to follow and emulate. Brown has listened and interacted with all groups to develop a systemwide commitment to exemplifying and integrating care and learning. This is clearly and consistently the spirit work that permeates the district.

How do powerful ideas come alive in day-to-day practice?

The Ithaca City School District is located in upstate New York and serves approximately 5,500 students, spread over 155 square miles and 12 schools. The Ithaca community is home to Cornell University, Ithaca College, and Tompkins Cortland Community College. The diverse student population is an equal mix of urban, suburban, and rural communities.

The school district's commitment to anti-racism has resulted in significant initiatives focused on revamping board of education policies, district curriculum, and instructional practices. Examples include the implementation of anti-marginalization units of study, de-tracking at middle schools and high schools, revision of the code of conduct, and transformation of grading and attendance practices.

Brown has received numerous awards and recognitions, including the 2017 New York State Superintendent of the Year, and is widely recognized as one of the nation's top educators and thought leaders. Brown had been recognized by the National School Boards Association with the prestigious Twenty to Watch Award and the Difference Maker Award. He also received the Center for Digital Education Top 30 Award and eSchool News Tech-Savvy Superintendent Award.

Brown is a highly regarded speaker and workshop facilitator, addressing a wide range of topics for local, regional, and national audiences. He has published numerous articles and is the author of *Culture of Love: Cultivating a Transformative and Positive Organizational Culture* (2018).

SPIRIT CONSTRUCTION IN ITHACA

A decade ago, Ithaca City School District was struggling: graduation rates were mediocre and academic proficiency was lagging in many areas, but in particular with low socioeconomic students, students with special needs, and students of color. Brown committed to addressing those needs not just by focusing on improving test scores but also on relationships, building trust, and conversations—lots of conversations. The work started with teachers, principals and administrators, parents and community leaders, and, most importantly, with students. As he put it, "We needed to build trust in each other, and that had to start with transparency and a whole lot of listening." Brown established his presence early and often in schools, classrooms, and the community. "We build trust by spending time together and learning from our conversations with each other." Focusing on cultural foundations soon resulted in a firm and emerging foundation based on trust and faith in each other. The superintendents' actions matched his words, and, in turn, the beginning work of spirit construction was taking stride.

Brown emphasized the need for openness and kindness toward each other. "We didn't look at this as a project or initiative, but as creating the conditions where students would learn best and teachers would thrive with their instructional endeavor." So often the prevailing work for school improvement is centered on test scores and misses the key to success for students and teachers: *relationships and trust*.

If we talk about faith and trust, it's natural to move on to talking about love within schools and classrooms. As we noted earlier, the word *love* is a tricky concept because it is used in so many ways, including superficially. Increasingly (and our book is a testament to this), the stakes for learning have become much more personal and emotional, given growing and extreme inequality and ambiguity about the future. The concepts of well-being and learning have become more closely connected. In the process, love—the way we use it as central to spirit work—is very much part of the emotions of learning to survive and thrive in the 21st century.

> "The district's evolution as a reflective organization has been key to the cultural growth and the emergence of a sense of spirit that lifts each of us." —**Dr. Luvelle Brown**

This significant spirit leadership work takes time and commitment. Leaders who understand the power of consistency embrace it with gusto. Ithaca teachers could see the value in a relational-based improvement effort, and early momentum could be felt by the Ithaca community. Brown suggests that the district's evolution as a reflective organization has been key to the cultural growth and the emergence of a sense of spirit that lifts each of us. Ithaca School District's policies have been modified to represent a caring, loving, and inclusive community. The culture has evolved with a constant focus on making sure students are heard and respected and that teachers are provided the resources and encouragement needed to succeed. As Brown notes, "We posted photographs of our students in the halls because we wanted them to know that they were 'home' in their school."

The school district in recent years has provided a level of focus to create a culture of love. This effort has resulted in policy changes that are representative of this effort. Discipline policies are now centered on corrective action and language rather than on punitive steps. Students and teachers are encouraged and supported in engaging in continuous dialogue about solving problems together and learning to work through issues. The district has embraced the voice of students as part of the decision-making process, and students serve on numerous committees as well as on the school board. Mary Grover, Ithaca School Distrct inclusion officer, put it this way: "Two years ago we made a commitment and priority to include students in the development of their individualized education plans (IEPs), and we invited them to be active members in their Committee of Special Education Meetings. The beauty of this is that we hear and listen directly to students about what they need, not just what we think they need. One student shared after one of the first meetings that they didn't like the idea that they had not been involved earlier." Ithaca School District is now working on being a nonracist culture and is involved in reflective work to end any racist or misogynistic practices.

When we observe the elements of spirit (trust, respect, love) and combine them with the consistent, thoughtful reflection that Ithaca City School District leaders and employees have embraced and utilized, it results in a prevailing sense of hope. "We believe in each other, and we believe in ourselves" is what one teacher said about the major result of the culture in Ithaca. In Chapter 7, we will pick up a theme that cuts across all our districts. Instead of handling misbehavior with escalating levels of punishment (that amounts to further and further exclusion), successful districts draw troubled students in with greater and greater mutual commitment. Supportive love and coordinated team effort have left an indelible mark on the Ithaca culture.

THE SCIENCE OF COLLABORATION

Fullan and Gallagher (2021) conclude that deep sustainable change across a school system happens when staff at all levels experience learning together (as is the case in Ithaca). We think of science as the study of life, so we believe that the science of collaboration is the study of the life of collaboration. Ithaca has created professional development that is built around collaborative enterprise. Brown elaborates (all quotes are from our interviews in 2021):

> We believe it is important to look beyond grades but to think forward to graduation and life. We are constantly fine-tuning collaborative practices, creating protocols and look-fors and then consistently utilizing teacher input to improve the entire process. When we hire teachers and principals, we are looking for those who embrace collaboration and are deeply vested as lifelong learners who believe in continuous improvement.

Brown continues:

> Students prefer to learn with other students and our best teachers are all about using this as a motivator to develop the learning mojo in classes. Ithaca has made a major effort over several years with professional development to grow their understanding of collaboration and what really works. They also believe that when students collaborate, it is an example of a relevance-forward phenomenon and is getting them ready for life and . . . they get it. Dialogue, conversations, and group and individual reflection are part of the foundation of our instructional practice. In most classrooms, you may not notice the teacher, because students help lead and engage the instruction to the level and needs of students.

As Brown states: "This doesn't happen overnight; we have spent years building capacity of both teachers and students to effectively grow the collaborative network in their classrooms."

This theme is echoed by Daniel Breiman, former ISD principal and district leader:

> Early in my work as a principal, teacher leaders suggested and promoted the idea of learning from peers as an essential instructional strategy. It was clear that teachers were ready and willing to break out of their classrooms and observe and learn from one another. The energy and spirit from joining forces to create shared knowledge and practices had an impact. Our faculty and the power of their collaboration helped me understand just how important peer-to-peer observation and reflection could be.

It is no coincidence that teachers who embrace collaborative and collegial work see their students do the same, and of course, the reverse is also true. Ithaca has developed digital resources in the district to provide each student a laptop and has employed a collaborative approach to professional development for effective use. This approach has been a key for students and teachers to know and experience learning together in a nurturing environment. Ithaca takes the success of their students very seriously and has improved learning outcomes for most students. The percent of students graduating has increased by 20% over several years and is now at 94%.

> Teachers who embrace collaborative and collegial work see their students do the same.

You don't see the constant focus on test results by the Ithaca team, but what you do see is learning improving and more and more students being successful. Luvelle Brown stresses, "We believe you teach happiness and a lot of that has to do with creating an environment where students' voices and choices are a major part of the work. Our focus is on getting students ready for life . . . not just a test." Ithaca has navigated the pandemic and school opening with a focus on transparency and community dialogue and input.

It is important to note that the deep sense of individual and collective spirit extends to all employees of the district. Recently, the district website featured a big tribute to the custodial and maintenance staff for their efforts to make sure every school is safe and clean. When employees know they are respected, they usually respond with spirit!

We interviewed Dr. Brown about his work. He asserted that the central driving force was love and that the core work is about changing culture. He called it "real equity work" (they have, in fact, mostly eliminated achievement gaps and increased success rates substantially). Brown has a grasp of what we call the "nuance of change" (Fullan, 2019). He said that what they are doing is hard work: "We connect in a loving way to do hard work." He captured one of the great insights about change leadership: "What we do is get specificity without imposing it." Brown showed a rare quality of understanding context while staying focused on mobilizing all groups and individuals to accomplish deep and lasting change in culture and related behaviors. The key words Brown uses to characterize the Ithaca culture include *honest, caring, trusting, selfless, forgiving, patient, committed.* Our mission, he stresses, "is what we do over and over again."

In sum, Ithaca is a district that has established love, respect, caring, and relationships as a key to its success. They have done this for a decade now, connecting it to learning, well-being, and overall success. Commitment to learning and to each other is deeply embedded: it shows in their values related, for example, to character and citizenship, and it shows in their success in completing high school as they proceed to postsecondary prospects.

VIRGINIA BEACH SCHOOLS

WHAT'S JOY GOT TO DO WITH IT?

In most vital organizations, there is a common bond of interdependence, mutual interest, interlocking contributions, and simple joy.

—*Leadership Is an Art* (Depree, 2004)

Virginia Beach Schools (VBS) understands the importance of joy and has focused a lot of effort and work to establish a culture and relationships that inculcate well-being and happiness among employees and students. Dr. Aaron Spence, appointed in 2014, has developed a leadership team and requisite systemic belief to build a new culture that would create an excellent place to work and learn. At the heart of the work in VBS is a constant focus on building the effectiveness and the ubiquitous nature of collaboration in the district. "We understand the importance and value of collaboration and devote time and energy to our effort to improve our work in this area," Spence shared with affirmation.

Dr. Aaron Spence

Virginia Beach Public Schools (VBPS) serves over 67,000 students in 86 different schools. This second-largest district in Virginia is a sprawling system that encompasses both urban and suburban areas and is adjacent to one of the largest military installations in the United States. The district appears to have been well managed over the years, with growing student enrollment and the need for additional schools and space. The area is a tourist attraction with its beaches and has prospered over the years with a focus on family and controlled growth. VBPS has been recognized as a national leader in digital innovation and has grown their resources for students and teachers over the last few years and provides a device for all students and teachers.

Spence previously served as superintendent of Moore County North Carolina Schools, where he led a major technology effort. He also served as assistant superintendent of Houston ISD. Earlier in his career, Spence was a principal in Henrico County, Virginia, and led one of the country's first one-to-one laptop programs at Deep Run High School. During his tenure at VBPS, every school received full accreditation for four years in a row; the graduation rate is at an all-time high. Spence was named the Virginia Superintendent of the Year in 2018 and the 2020 Digital Superintendent of the Year by the Consortium for School Networking. In 2021, he was named the AASA National Digital Superintendent of the Year. Spence grew up in Virginia Beach and his commitment to and for the community stems in part from his reflection of what the school system meant to him over the years. The district's recent leadership focus has been on equity and innovation, as exemplified by VBPS's partnership with the Chesapeake Foundation Environmental Education.

SCAFFOLDING SPIRIT WORK

Virginia Beach Schools leaders emphasize three things that they want for all students:

1. To be cared for emotionally
2. To learn every day
3. To be loved

Aaron Spence and the Virginia Beach team have led with a focus on building trust and a sense of community. "I tell our leaders I love them every day. We have to lift each other. Our actions must reflect our beliefs. Teachers are respected and loved," Spence shares as keys to spirit scaffolding.

> We have utilized Teacher Forums to focus on listening. It sounds simple enough, but we have to respond with action to what we hear, to solve problems. We also take this opportunity and others to constantly affirm the work of our teachers and to lift them up. We use our daily interactions to recognize teachers who are leading and to promote their work in our schools and classrooms.

Another aspect of building the cultural structure of the district is embracing the importance of talking to one another. "I visit every school every year and walk around with the principal. My work is centered on listening and affirming the principal, teachers, students, and employees. Our central office and school leaders have employed similar daily efforts and we keep this ongoing dialogue about our work and how we are doing." With the challenge of the pandemic and the importance of clear information, Spence initiated "desk chats" where he would Zoom cast an update for the entire staff and offer straight talk from the heart about what was going on. "Sure, we have bumps and some bruises getting through the challenges of virtual instruction and when and how to reopen, but we have to keep working on it. We have to."

Conviction is one of the attributes that Spence seeks in all VBPS leaders to demonstrate as role models. He stresses that "caring and loving for students undergirds everything we do. Everything! We have high expectations for students and adults and believe that it is a key to school improvement. We have to know our kids, really know them. We have to know their names. Students need to hear their names from all teachers. We know that relationships are vital. As we struggle with difficult challenges, we need each other more than ever before. We need everybody's creativity and caring and open hearts to find our way through. We can help one another by trusting and believing in each other. We can't get there alone, we can't get there without each other." Such deep commitment reminds us of the core of Meg Wheatley's work (Wheatley, 2009).

> "We can help one another by trusting and believing in each other. We can't get there alone; we can't get there without each other." —**Dr. Aaron Spence**

TRUST AND FAITH

Relationships are at the heart of VBPS classrooms and the single most important ingredient in building trust and, ultimately, faith in each other. Spence emphasizes,

> Our students need to have a great day, every day. We have to start each day with that sense that "we can make it happen today." We have morning meetings in our classrooms to get to know each other but also to build belief in one another. We want our classrooms to be responsive to students. We are learning how to get to know each other and to build connections not as some ancillary thing, but as one of the most important things we do. We have to leverage this time to our collective good.

Fullan describes this as *nuanced leadership*: "Nuanced leaders are obsessed with making an impact . . . they unlock, mobilize, and create collective care" (2019). VBPS leaders have become thoughtful and creative in their efforts to create conversations and trust with families. With the challenge of the pandemic, Green Run High School leaders were initiating "family voice" to use conversations to build relationships and communication. Family Voice Empowerment Groups (small chat rooms) became a true evolution of collaboration with families, students, and our outreach staff. Spence states that

> Our goal is to create safe and sustainable dialogue with families where they can share concerns, needs, or ideas. We focus on listening to understand our families. We analyze trends as a catalyst for improvements and problem solving.

> As our Family Voice Groups have grown in number, we are reminded of the need for patience and perseverance, which are key ingredients to our trust-building efforts. These relationships are not built overnight, but rather one conversation at a time. Through consistency and shared vulnerability, we are creating conditions for sharing and trusting. When our families feel loved, encouraged, and respected, they understand that their voices matter and will be heard. Leslie Riccio and Rachel Thompson are leading this work with conviction for VBPS families.

The relentless consistency is key to VBPS's success:

> To build on trust and to create faith in each other, we have to step up and do what we say. We have to demonstrate our efforts to grow our community and to value every employee. We have worked hard at developing meaningful professional development and modeling how we want to treat each other as we learn and grow together. Humor and laughter are vital parts of our classrooms and schools. We have to stay human, poke fun at ourselves, and have fun. Smiling and laughter should be prevalent in schools and classrooms. Students want to have fun when they are learning and they really do like to learn with each other. They understand that if a teacher has a sense of spirit (trust, faith, laughter), they are in a good place to learn. Virginia Beach Schools has established Joy Ambassadors to promote joy in schools. What does joy have to do with schools . . . ? Everything, in good schools.

SCIENTISTS OF COLLABORATION

Virginia Beach gets that collaboration is key. Spence explains,

> We have established a culture of collaboration that took years to create. Teachers, students, specialists, and administrators coach each other up about collaboration. We use design principles to solve problems and part of those design

> principles is a focus on continuous improvement. We have continuous dialogue about how students learn in classrooms and how they learn with one another and, most importantly, how we learn together as educators.

The work of collaboration science never ends and needs constant nurturance, as do all living things. Investing heavily in developing staff to build capacity, focusing on skills and dispositions that help people collaborate, and promoting the need for continuous learning and reflection are part of a proven formula (see also Fullan & Edwards, 2017). Spence notes that

> Personal reflection on our experience is how we learn. Reflection contributes to the refinement of subsequent action and the building of professional craft and knowledge. And, of course, reflecting on practice—by observing practice, by writing about practice, by engaging in conversation about practice, by embracing the differences we encounter in practice—builds a school culture hospitable to both learning and community.

Once again, we note that spirit work and collaboration are heavily grounded in specific day-to-day work. Casey Conger, principal of Cooke Elementary, shares how spirit work is built into daily interaction:

> Cooke staff have created four houses that correspond with the four pillars of the district: respect, kindness, responsibility, and safety. Every staff member and every student are members of a house where they lead efforts to promote and contribute to the spirit and hope for everyone. When you are a new student at Cooke, the minute you walk into the class, students are cheering you on. In a school community that is over 50% transient, creating a space where students feel seen, accepted, and valued is an absolute top priority.

In collaborative cultures, educators plan, teach, assess, and reflect on a constant basis. One of the first lessons of collaborative science is that everyone is a teacher, and everyone is a student learning from one another. Spence stresses that in such cultures, it is crystal clear that students need to learn with each other. He notes that they "have looked at learning landscape and have built collaborative spaces to enhance how we work, and to support collaborative endeavors." In the last couple of years, the district has focused on deeper learning concepts: students define their learning goals and their dispositions (working with one another and listening) and balance this with academic goals. The ultimate focus is on students becoming learning leaders. Spence notes, "The new pedagogies goal is for students to become independent learners who manage and design the learning process effectively."

There has been considerable success since their journey began in 2014. The norm of "specific introspection" is firmly embedded and reinforced daily: as Spence says, "When we meet with our teacher forum, we use breakout groups for dialogue, collaboration, sharing and being vulnerable, and for coaching. We understand we have a lot to learn, and we have decided to do it together." Once more, we see that spirit and collaboration are explicit, feed on each other, and are continually practiced.

Finally, we see in Virginia Beach the dynamic role of the pandemic. As we have observed in other situations, organizations that had strong spirit values and related collaborative cultures from the start were much more able to handle the disruption. In the case of VBPS, the spirit culture strength also led to even deeper innovation for the future. This became clear in an interview we did with Superintendent Spence, who starts by saying, "If you like leadership and enjoy the muck and morass of leadership, then this past year was for you." He continues, "I mentor folks around the country in leadership, and I realized that leaders are or should be built for these moments of crisis. Emotionally, it is really draining, and the collaborative piece we had served us well. From Day 1, on March 13, 2020, when the governor announced school closure, you knew that this was going to be different."

Organizations that had strong spirit values and related collaborative cultures from the start were much more able to handle the disruption.

Spence describes in some detail what happened:

> We began immediately with our senior team, and met every day (virtually), seven days a week for six months. As we were meeting, we began to realize the typical hierarchical leadership, even when it is consultative, would not work. Decisions had to be made so quickly, and the issues were so complex, we needed everyone's best thinking and we needed it all the time. We expanded beyond the senior team and put 40 to 60 people in the Zoom room, seven days a week for several months, until we realized we were burning people out. But the beautiful part of that is that we had deconstructed the hierarchy with many more people at all levels, getting a say about the best decisions in the moment. Because we had a strong collaborative culture to begin with, we did not lose control as we extended collaboration. It became a regular check-in about who needs to put something on the table.

Again, as we are seeing in other cases, it is not just that collaborative cultures cope better in the short run, but also that *after the extreme pressure of the pandemic, people do not want to go back to the old ways.* Rather, they want to innovate! They want to go beyond what they were doing in pre-COVID-19 days. "We need a retreat," says Spence. "What have we started doing better that has proven to be a strength, that we need to keep? What can we do without and need to drop? We are going to have to be a lot more flexible than ever before as we assess proof-of-concept."

Spence went on to say that he worries about people who are focusing only on learning loss, as in a deficit model. He says it has become much clearer how to organize learning in context:

"Once you put your core values in order you can focus on basic skills in literacy and numeracy, and then organize content in a way that accelerates learning."

In short, spirit work and related collaboration put you in good stead all the time and soon lead to the press for more effective innovation. Spirit and collaboration are *generative capacities*. They keep on giving, all the more so in times of difficulty.

ROWAN-SALISBURY SCHOOL SYSTEM (NORTH CAROLINA)

Dr. Lynn Moody

HERE WE GROW!

In collaboration with other teachers and instructional leaders, the teacher is constantly monitoring and making adjustments. The teacher has to be more, not less, creative than in traditional teaching . . . he or she is now engaged in intentional mindfulness.

—*The Six Secrets of Change* (Fullan, 2008)

Rowan-Salisbury School System has embraced becoming a learning organization in which students are respected and have a clear voice in the instructional process. Superintendent Dr. Lynn Moody—appointed in 2014, retired in 2020—has provided opportunities for teachers and administrators to "go and grow" with visits to other school districts to find the best examples available to learn from. Rowan-Salisbury Schools leaders have evolved with nuanced dispositions, meaning that they

1. See their role as a leader in a broad manner that extends outside of the school.
2. Understand their role as being part of a variety of external networks.
3. Develop abilities to engage others inside and outside the school in partnerships.
4. Use technology to expand and manage a network of resources. (Fullan, 2019)

The district has faced some significant learning deficiencies for students and has recently adopted a renewal system to focus attention and effort on improvement and recognizing students for their unique talents as well as all teachers for their leadership.

The Rowan-Salisbury School District serves around 20,000 students, K–12, in Salisbury, North Carolina. The district has 37 schools and employs over 3,000 staff members. The district has a 65% poverty rate of students and has experienced a growth of diversity in recent years. The community is about 20 miles northeast of Charlotte, North Carolina, and has rural, suburban, and some urban elements in the community demographics. Without significant industry, the local economy has suffered, and significant numbers of families struggle to make ends meet.

Moody previously served as superintendent of Rock Hill, South Carolina, School District and led a significant technology effort there to provide each student with their own digital device. As she started her work in Rowan-Salisbury, one of her first major initiatives was to provide all students digital access with their own devices. The digital divide and a lack of equity for student resources made this a priority—one that the community embraced. Moody knew the district had much work to do to improve student success and teacher productivity, and she initiated a new focus on professional development. As the district grew the efforts to enhance academic performance, Moody focused on building the culture and inculcating a new team spirit and trust:

> We believe our community deserves an education system with schools that are encouraged to create an engaging and personalized learning environment where students and teachers enjoy their work. In our schools, teachers are treated like the experts they are. We want our teachers to be leaders, designers, and creators of instruction.

Building professional trust is foundational to the district. Moody set out to demonstrate the conviction that everyone matters and that their respective voices must be heard: "When teachers know you really listen to them . . . then they usually will listen to you. The idea of shared and participatory leadership is the direction we are going in. Building trust and a shared spirit about the work is not a position to be adopted, but begins with a deep belief in the potential of each other." Moody stresses that "this kind of trust or spirit building comes from our hearts and out of our collective philosophy about people."

> "Building trust and a shared spirit about the work is not a position to be adopted but begins with a deep belief in the potential of each other." —**Dr. Lynn Moody**

With the pandemic, the district had a real divide about when and how to open school, but in the end, pulled together and made it work. Moody attributes the successful transition to the collective and problem-solving capacity that the district developed over the past six years: "We are continuing to learn and grow how to problem solve and how to get things done. Over the years we have built in time for dialogue, time to talk things over, figuring out what we believe, and time to know each other as professionals." A good example of connecting spirit to collaboration is described by Dr. Kelly Withers, who served as principal at South Rowan High School:

> We had the good fortune of having our leadership team travel to observe several outstanding models in several different states. We planned time for our team to reflect and have discussions about building our vision for the school and our understanding and commitment to collaboration. We had great discussions and spirited debates but evolved with a clear understanding of our mutual belief and love for our students and love for each other.

As Margaret Wheatley (2002) has stated, "Human conversation is the most ancient and easiest way to cultivate the conditions for change, personal change, community change, and organizational change. If we can sit together and talk about what's important to us, we begin to come alive." Rowan-Salisbury staff have studied a lot of districts and other communities and have embraced some cultural standards to guide the work with all students. Moody observes, "We know academic success for each student is a must and have to dedicate ourselves to each student's learning. Interpersonal skills are equally important, and we focus on creativity, leadership, teamwork, civility, work ethic, communication, and problem solving. We also are emphasizing unique life goals for each student and ask them to think about their personal passions and life aspirations. We have had hundreds of conversations with teachers to create a sense of family and to build a sense of faith in each other."

Moody shares a story about a student in Rowan-Salisbury Schools who was part of the evolving spirit culture:

> Sampson was a special needs student who was mentored by a custodian in his school in a career technical education

(CTE) work experience class. He had the opportunity to work side by side with the custodian and others. His mentor was kind and encouraging, which motivated Sampson to work hard and learn some skills. When he graduated, his principal recommended that he be hired as a custodian. I had met him a few times when he was a student, and invited him to a community breakfast and asked him to sit in the front row. He told me he was so excited to be invited to the breakfast that he went to the Goodwill Store and bought a suit to wear. He brought me a decorative candle that he had asked some students to sign to thank me. A few months later, we had an employee discussion group and he attended. Afterward, he came up to me and said he wanted to share something with me. He said that he and his custodian colleagues would like to have shirts like the maintenance team had. He also shared that the steel-toed work boots were almost $75, and they couldn't afford them. He said his work friends knew he had a connection with the superintendent and she needed to know. Sampson said, "They helped me and so I wanted to help." Sampson's experience led to the custodians receiving the shirts they wanted and to a local store that offered the boots for less than $25.

A large number of Rowan-Salisbury students come from tough environments. The district has worked to establish a clear understanding that they have to look at the total well-being of students. Teaching good health and personal wellness is taken seriously. The district has worked explicitly at overcoming punitive compared to supportive reactions to problems. Therese Pierce, Rowan Teacher of the Year, notes that "When you go to the doctor, you want a personalized diagnosis. That is what we are doing for every student, personalizing their education." Moody and the leadership team recognized a lack of progress in student academic success and the need for serious work and direction. Even after a major focus on academics and data review, student academic performance remained flat for several years and below the state average in most areas. One significant bright spot had been a small but consistent improvement in the graduation rate over the last several years, rising to 85%. The Rowan-Salisbury Schools decided to embark on a new and innovative systemic approach to teaching and learning that would move from a primary focus on testing and academics to a renewal directional system in 2018. The renewal system identifies three areas of focus for student success:

1. Interpersonal skills with a focus on communication, teamwork, creativity, and civility
2. Unique life goals with personal and career interests as the key drivers
3. Academic skills integrated with analyzing and solving real-world problems

This sense of encompassing spirit work extends beyond the classroom and beyond instructional staff. Dr. Jason Gardner, assistant superintendent, shares a great example of the merger of spirit and collaboration with support staff leaders stepping up. The school nutrition and transportation staff brainstormed about a way to support students during the summer and came up with the advent of the Yum Yum Bus, which traveled to families and communities in need. Child nutrition director Lisa Altman describes the work:

> The bus distributed meals and books as well as other curriculum materials for students and families. There were also abundant hugs and smiles for students. Seeing our school nutrition staff reach out to help meant so much. Seeing the smiles and happiness of our families when the Yum Yum Bus would arrive was an inspiration to many and confirmation of our spirit and love for our students.

We mentioned that Superintendent Moody retired in 2020. We asked her what she had learned about leadership and learning. First, she said, "it is essential to identify, connect with, and listen to the people you work with; then it is much easier to lead." And that "if you don't take the time to connect in the first place, you will have to trudge through most things. You can't really lead people until they want to be led by you."

On another dimension, we got the impression that Moody wished that she was just starting her career, having concluded that certain innovations in learning are needed. "Now that I am retired," she said, "I have time to think about learner-centered design. Students need to develop their passions, interests, and their unique talents in this world . . . there should be a lot less standardizing children."

CONCLUSION

As we study these eight districts, we think that the combination of spirit and collaboration, plus the COVID-19 disruption and its fallout, have put innovation and system change on the table—a theme we will take up in the final chapter. Our main conclusion remains: certain districts are discovering that going deep into spirit and collaboration is essential for the short run, and may be the best route for even deeper transformation.

Let's extend this proposition to two large districts.

5 SOUTH CENTRAL DISTRICTS (UNITED STATES) IN ACTION

We now turn south for two large school districts: Shelby County Schools in Memphis, Tennessee, and Jefferson County in Louisville, Kentucky. Spirit work and the science of collaboration travel well because they apply to any school system committed to serving all its students. In each of the three chapters, and their eight associated districts in Part II, we learn more about our two key themes because we see them manifested under different conditions. We learn about the concepts because their role is exemplified in each case. We become all the more clear about their nature and how they operate under very different circumstances.

SHELBY COUNTY SCHOOLS (TENNESSEE)

HEART OF THE MID-SOUTH

The heart of leadership is in the hearts of leaders. You have to lead from something deep in your heart. Trusting people to solve problems generates higher levels of motivation and better solutions.

—*Leading With Soul* (Bolman & Deal, 2011)

Shelby County Schools (SCS) is the largest district in Tennessee and serves more than 104,000 students in 200 schools. The district has over 14,000 employees and is the second-largest employer in the county. The district includes the city of Memphis, with its rich cultural heritage. Seventy-four percent of the students qualify for federal subsistence due to poverty. Eighty percent of the students are Black, and the district serves both a very large urban population and suburban and rural areas. The University of Memphis and FedEx corporate headquarters are both located in Memphis. Recently the district has focused on five key areas: (1) early literacy, (2) post-secondary readiness, (3) developing teachers, leaders, and support staff, (4) expanding school options, and (5) working closely with families and with community partners to support their schools.

Superintendent Dr. Joris Ray ("Dr. Ray," as he is called by all) was appointed superintendent of Shelby County Schools in 2019. He proudly says he is a "home-grown leader." He earned his doctoral degree from the University of Memphis and is a graduate of the 2019 Harvard Institute for Superintendents. He served in the district for 23 years as a teacher, principal, director, assistant superintendent, and chief of academic operations prior to being named the superintendent. Ray has immense pride in SCS and embraces servant leadership, seeing his work as lifting and leading all students and all employees. He has a knowledge of the community, and the community knows and respects him. Ray has a competent and dedicated group of leaders who he has fired up with a sense of belief in each other. SCS recognizes the need to grow and improve and has developed a collective disposition of determination and efficacy for every student.

Dr. Ray

BUILDING TRUST

Shelby County Schools have been deliberate and consistent with their focus to build trust with teachers, parents, community members, and, most of all, with students. "It begins with being transparent and vulnerable," stresses Ray. "We have to be real and authentic in our leadership. We have to lead with our hearts—leading with heart work and hard work." The district leaders recognize that the district has much room for improvement in several areas, but the focus is on building the foundation with trust and communication. Ray is naturally enthusiastic and implores leaders to model the behaviors that they want to see: "We have to make this a great place to work for teachers and a great place to learn for students. Every day, in every way, we have to focus our work on students and teachers."

> "We have to be real and authentic in our leadership. We have to lead with our hearts—leading with heart work and hard work." —**Dr. Ray**

Shelby County Schools are constantly engaged in an array of community support programs for parents' resources and other assistance. Extending help to families builds trust and communication, and SCS excels at this—what we are calling *spirit work*. Ruby Richmond serves as the SCS district receptionist and was born and raised in Memphis and has long been a spirit leader: "I have reflected on going to school in Memphis City Schools and how much it meant to me and how grateful I am to represent as a legacy member of the SCS team." Ruby considers her work a ministry. "I greet strangers every day with love and sincere interest in listening. We never get a second chance to make a first impression. You never know what kind of day someone is having, and we must show up with SCS spirit."

When asked about his leadership style, Ray called himself a "servant leader." This can be a superficial concept that leaders can claim, but what does it mean on a daily basis? Ray talks about building a team that gets the work done; there is no job too big or too small. Ray refers to establishing a climate "where everyone is being respectful, which I demand of everyone. My motto is 'Take care of yourself, take care of your family, and take care of your team.'"

LOVE IS ALIVE

We have noted from time to time in this book that *love* can be perceived as a kind of mushy concept. And maybe a lot of leaders do use it superficially. We have gone to some trouble in this book to look more deeply across the cases, and we feel confident that the emotional commitment from the leaders is deep and is seen to be so by students, educators, and families in the districts. Moreover, the leaders have developed such commitment with other internal leaders at the district and school levels that they have established a *culture of care* in the districts as a whole. As we noted in Chapter 1, the pandemic has made it normal to show love literally under life-and-death circumstances. What could represent a more poignant opportunity than helping all kids succeed in new education that helps them "engage the world change the world" (Fullan et al., 2018; Quinn et al., 2020)?

So what we see in this very large high poverty district is love and care, Memphis style. Ray and Shelby County staff are constantly sending messages of care and love to students and family, as he explains to us:

> It is essential that we pay attention to and understand the social and emotional needs of children. Many of our students come from great adversity and need to be loved . . . first. When students are hurting or live with fear, then we must provide the love, care, and sense of belonging that may be absent in their lives. We have to show our teachers that we love them and care about them if we want them to love our students. Earlier this year, we made the

> decision that it was not safe to play football this year due to the pandemic, and there was a significant outcry and anger.

At a public hearing on the matter, the superintendent was facing heat and obvious frustration from community members. Ray went to the podium and spoke with conviction: "I love Memphis sports . . . and have my whole life. But I love our student-athletes more."

There was no question Ray was speaking from his heart, and the community members recognized it. The school district is cognizant of the multiple constituencies that must be acknowledged as part of the team and family and communicates respect for community members. Margaret Wheatley puts it best in her book *A Simple Way*:

> Organizations can keep searching for new ties that will bind them together . . . new incentives, rewards, or policies; but organizations can accomplish much more if they rely on passions evoked when we connect to others, purpose to purpose.

Yolanda Martin, who serves as Chief of Human Resources for SCS, describes the spirit of SCS work:

> We work to honor and support employees throughout their careers. When we asked our teachers to all go virtual, we mobilized to offer support in every way we could. We understand that it takes care and commitment to motivate and sustain our workforce. We launched SCS Cares as a foundational platform to recognize and honor employees in a variety of ways throughout the year. We send the message every day that "We care about you, and we are with you" to all employees.

When Ray found out that he had been selected as superintendent of Shelby County Schools, he was excited to share the news with his father. "Just always remember to keep your focus on students and teachers" is what Ray's dad said upon hearing the news. The superintendent took his father's words seriously and has used that advice every day to guide his work. In his first months as superintendent, Ray worked with the leadership team to establish a Parent Welcome Center to provide information, support, and services to parents and community members. Every week, the district confirms its personalized commitment by providing services and support for families and students in need. A wide variety of efforts are directed at vulnerable families who need food, clothing, and other assistance. It's not just about academics—it's about supporting families and their needs and sending a clear message of care and love to the community. Ray explains,

> Our professional development includes guiding design about how we treat each other and how we treat our students. We talk about the "SCS Way"—compassion for everyone. We know we often fall short and need to show grace. Our caring means we are accountable to each other and the community, and we emphasize being servant leaders and caring about all employees as human beings. The message is clear: "Respect people."

As Depree has stressed in *Leadership Is an Art*, "Respect begins with an understanding of the diversity of people's gifts. Understanding the diversity of these gifts enables us to begin the crucial step of trusting each other" (Depree, 2004).

COLLABORATIVE EVOLUTION

Ray and the SCS Leadership Cabinet look at their work through the lens of solving problems of practice. "We are constantly discussing and reflecting as a team about our work, and how to improve it. The district has embraced the disposition that one of the main jobs of all leaders is to develop and mentor other leaders. We recognize the importance of informal conversations and see that as planting seeds and watering . . . the garden of leadership." Incidentally, it is remarkable in the eight districts how many times we encountered the presence of mentoring of leaders, including named mentors for each of the superintendents in our sample—a topic we return to in the final chapter.

As the pandemic was spreading in the spring of 2020, SCS leadership was working with great urgency to face the myriad of challenges ahead. As Ray puts it, "We did three years' work in eight weeks." The district provided each of the 100,000 students with their own personal devices as well as internet connectivity. This was a monumental challenge that required tremendous team analysis and planning. Ray and the SCS school board proceeded by naming a Digital Planning Team who would recommend the devices to be selected for student use. This was a significant decision in that the message was clear to the entire community: SCS, with a new superintendent in Ray, would embrace a significant collaborative process to make these huge decisions. The SCS Device Selection Committee included school leaders, teachers, students, SCS school board members, Memphis business and community leaders, and other elected officials. The large and diverse committee realized the urgency at hand and worked through differences and debates to make every effort and best decision in a timely manner. That didn't mean that the initial challenges of using a truly collaborative process didn't create some noise to work through. Ray told a compelling story at one of the early committee meetings about how, as a high school student in Memphis in Shelby County, he received a graphing calculator from his high school for his personal use. "We could not afford a graphing calculator and we were very appreciative, and I have not forgotten what that meant to me and my family. It's now our time to stand up together for our students today."

There was plenty of debate and a big dose of what SCS leaders call "healthy noise" throughout the process. Ray refers to this productive noise as "brother-and-sister tension while we figure things out." Collaborative work is challenging, and finding the way to pull together after strong, even fierce, debate requires maturity of dispositions. During one discussion/debate about how to move forward with the acquisition of devices, one member of the committee challenged the direction the committee was going with the initiative to provide each student with their own device and addressed Ray directly. "Are you willing to put your job on the line for this decision to provide every student a device?" the local leader asked Ray. Ray looked directly at the individual asking and responded, "I put my job on the line every day for the students of Shelby County . . . that's what I do." The committee appreciated the debate and appreciated even more the superintendent's stand-up conviction for students. The decision was clear in the end: equity and well-being of every student was the path forward. Every member of the committee was invited to provide input, and the tone of mutual respect set the culture of the meetings. With new leadership, SCS was moving forward with a powerful message: *We can make the best decisions if we use a variety of voices to lead the process to find the best way forward. We acknowledge one another as equals, remain interested in hearing others' views, and recognize that we need each other and that we need to learn to reflect together—that we expect it to be messy, and that conversation is the natural way humans think together* (see Wheatley, 2009). SCS Chief of Business Operations Genard Phillips describes the effect of the growing collaborative spirit:

> Every day I work with colleagues as we plan and then take action to make a difference for our students and their families. We trust in our superintendent and he trusts us, and we have a shared vision about our work. Even on the operations side, we are clear that our work is about improving graduation rates and improving literacy and success for all students.

SCS leaders are taking significant strides down the road of collaborative evolution and are committed to learning as a team. In addition to the Digital Planning Committee, another team was formed, the Digital Deployment Committee, to guide the process of the deployment of the devices as well as configuring the internet connectivity design to ensure every student had connectivity at home. These two efforts to support students (device and connectivity) could be described as the greatest steps toward equity for all students in the last fifty years in Memphis.

This was a massive undertaking and incredibly complicated, with huge urgency and plenty of unknowns. The process included lots of healthy noise and a measure of tension and sometimes raucous debate as the team waded through the planning to make sure every student would be equipped for the opening of school, even in virtual settings. As we said in a previous book, *Unstoppable Momentum*, "Achieving success in implementing technology in education is like an iceberg. The technology is clearly visible, but below the surface is something much larger that really counts. This something is where we find deep learning, a melding of skills and attributes that range from critical thinking and problem solving to citizenship and creativity" (Fullan & Edwards, 2017).

The SCS's digital deployment went incredibly well. There were bumps and the challenges are ongoing, but the goals were met and new learning of how to get things done was emerging. "At the heart of the cultural change that is needed to move a system forward to actually achieve improved results is the move to purposeful collaboration" (Fullan & Gallagher, 2020).

Spirit and collaboration have been the heart of the great work going on at Berclair Elementary School, led by Principal Sam Shaw. Berclair serves a highly diverse community where most children come from economically depressed homes. Arabic, Hispanic, Black, and several other subsets compose the student population. Berclair has achieved the highest rating a school in Tennessee can achieve, a level 5, and it is recognized as a Tennessee Reward School for ranking in the top 5% of all schools in Tennessee. These achievements were accomplished over time by many people working together with great passion, love, and commitment for their students.

As Shaw notes, "Our faculty has a rich history of embracing each other to build a strong collaborative culture for our students. Concepts like equity, love, faith, and servant leadership have been thrust into the forefront of our education work in Shelby County."

LOOKING AHEAD

More radical changes lie ahead. As we were finalizing this chapter, the local paper, *The Commercial Appeal*, reported on SCS's new re-imagining plan (Testino, 2021). The plan includes changing the name of the district to "Memphis Shelby Schools," restructuring some schools to include kindergarten classes for all four-year-olds, closing and merging other schools, and several changes for each grade band for elementary, middle, and high schools, including expanding outdoor learning spaces, developing emotional intelligence courses at all levels, preparing students to work in the global economy, creating theater and visual arts, and more.

In introducing the radical and comprehensive plans, Ray stated, "Coronavirus will not defeat us; today will be my last time repeating that phrase. . . . We are stronger together. We are resilient" (quoted in *The Commercial Appeal*). Both superintendent Ray and John Barker, Deputy Superintendent of Finance and Operations, stressed that the new plans and the federal money to support them are "game changing."

As authors of this book and as leaders who have experienced large-scale fundamental reform, we find that the scope of these changes is breathtaking. We know that the longevity of superintendents in given roles can be limited (Ray is heading into his third year). We also know that cultures with depth—spawning leaders at all levels with deep and specific spirit along with focused collaborative capacities—establish legacies that serve as platforms for continuity and depth. Such cultures and structures may be just what is needed in post-pandemic times. Deep concepts enable bold moves!

Cultures with depth—spawning leaders at all levels with deep and specific spirit along with focused collaborative capacities—establish legacies that serve as platforms for continuity and depth.

Finally, we note again that strong leaders not only rise to the occasion when there are major crises, but they also use the disruption to make deep positive transformational reform that perhaps should have been made earlier. Adapting an observation from one of our colleagues, Lyle Kirtman, the question is: "Do you want to be a manager of COVID-19 or a leader of the organization?"

JEFFERSON COUNTY PUBLIC SCHOOLS (KENTUCKY)

POSITIVITY PREVAILS

Spirit. The internal force that sustains meaning and hope.

—*Leading With Soul* (Bolman & Deal, 2011)

Louisville, Kentucky, is known for horse racing and the excitement and energy of that kind of event. Jefferson County Public Schools (which includes Louisville) have been experiencing some of their own excitement and challenge in the effort to provide every student access to digital resources and to prepare every student for life. Their relative success is only recent, so we have a chance in this case to examine how a large district can transform from failing to succeeding in a fairly short period.

Jefferson County Public Schools (JCPS) is the largest district in Kentucky and the twenty-ninth largest in the country, with 96,000 students and 150 schools. The diverse district has struggled historically with zoning, bussing, and integration

Dr. Marty Pollio

issues. The majority of students (60%) are non-white, and 66% qualify for free or reduced -price lunch. The greater Jefferson County includes urban, suburban, and rural areas. In 2017, a study of the district indicated that immediate action was needed to ensure equity for all students and to avoid resegregation. The study called for new leadership and change. Louisville University has been an active partner with JCPS over the years and is a major presence in the community. The business community is deeply involved with JCPS, having established over 135 partnerships in association with JCPS career technical education programs. But things were not going well, and by 2016, there was talk of the state taking over the district.

You could call Dr. Marty Pollio, the current leader, the "surprise superintendent." He grew up professionally in JCPS. He was a basketball coach, then an assistant principal, and later a principal of one of the high schools. He was then asked by the board to take over a second high school that was the second-lowest performing school in the state. He was assigned what would be called "a turnaround mandate." At the same time, the district as a whole was performing poorly in a culture of low morale and a kind of bunker mentality. Pollio later called Louisville a "system of schools," not a "school system"—operating as 150 independent contractors working in isolation. By 2017, as things were worsening, the state board was considering taking over the district. The Louisville School Board itself did not renew the contract of the superintendent at the time. Pollio was appointed an acting superintendent in 2017, and eight months later, on April 1, 2018, was named superintendent.

One of our recent sticky phrases is *Go slow to go fast*. The "go slow" part is to have a small number of powerful drivers that become shared at the front end of the change process. When an organization has been unsuccessful over time, there is usually limited energy and little sense that change is possible. The start of a new direction is tricky. If the situation is bad, as was the case with JCPS, the expectation must be that major change is essential. A process must be set in a way that the leader makes clear that they will work with other leaders to start and build in a new direction. There are common principles to successful change processes, but they vary in detail according to context. These commonalities must be nuanced to the situation and the associated dynamic interaction, especially in the early stages. We interviewed Superintendent Pollio to get to some of the details (which we could, in turn, verify with others). In this way we were able to get at the details of JCPS's success story.

Pollio started the interview by saying that the culture of the district was so damaged that there was no sense of direction. He noted that "leadership is always grounded in giving people 'a purpose and a sense of why.'" He continued by noting that people need a North Star—a *why*. "I am a leader in positivity. I tell everyone we must be human—we must be human lighthouses for children." Pollio then makes a series of key points: "When you reach a tipping point, when the majority of people start working with a positive lens, magic happens. Leaders need to state what values they stand for, and then back it up every single day not just with words, but with actions."

"When you reach a tipping point, when the majority of people start working with a positive lens, magic happens." —**Dr. Marty Pollio**

We suspect that the culture began to shift partly because of the persistent and widespread negativity in the district, and partly because Pollio had a positive plan that attracted other leaders. The new image of purpose consisted of three pillars:

1. Positive school climate and trust
2. Racial equality
3. "Backpack of Skills" (more about this later)

In the beginning, there is certainly a degree of top-down assertiveness operating here. Pollio describes it as giving direction about purpose and then enabling school leaders to take the helm and shape it to evolve in their school.

The question of turnover is tricky, and here we find Jim Collins's (2001) concept of "flywheel" applicable. The physics of the flywheel is that once momentum is established, for better or worse (in this case, for better), all you need to do is keep flicking or feeding the flywheel in order to maintain and increase its momentum. In concrete terms, you start by naming and seeking a positive culture; you support people to work in teams; the teams begin to get degrees of success; good people find that they want to stay in such a culture; word gets around that your organization is a good place to work, so more good people become attracted to join the organization; new people join and become incorporated into teams; and on it goes.

Pollio as much as defined the flywheel without using the term. He noted that there was no leadership development program in the district when he took over. He says,

> First, you have to hire and promote from within. Then you need to use a mixture of inside and outside hiring and promotion decisions, which at first created tension, but once the process gets going, became more valued. We had several people come back to Jefferson who had left. We promoted from within and attracted people from all over the state and the nation who wanted to work at Jefferson.

Building a new central team according to the new agenda was key. School leadership began to change. Over the past three years, there has been a significant turnover in the principalship (some 70% of school principals are new). What Pollio is talking about is the sense of new spirit, where he worked relentlessly to establish the deep *why* and what it entailed. In our own model in this book, we see spirit and collaboration feeding on one another. Once in place, the two phenomena become virtually fused. Schools vary, but Pollio believes that each school can have a sense of ownership within the school and community and in relation to the district. When this happens, he notes, you can feel such an identity—students, teachers, parents feel it too. The reverse is also true: when we don't own it, we all know it. Pollio and his team set out to build and develop individual and team conviction. Coaching and feedback are a big part of JCPS's development. It's beyond just caring or loving them into success. It is part and parcel of the instructional vision for the district. Pollio stresses that they strive to be simple and straightforward with fidelity, authenticity, and care and love of students.

CREATING A SPIRIT OF TRUST

Pollio reflects on how to build a sense of spirit. He emphasizes that it all begins with trust. Every leader must start with building trust as part of who they are and what they do. Every teacher, principal, and administrator must embrace daily work on building trust, hope, and a sense of spirit. Pollio elaborates on the strategy:

> Understanding local nuance and being steadfastly transparent are things we have to work on day in and day out. It is important that we celebrate growth but that we also acknowledge shortcomings as a team and family. Ultimately, we want to create a sense of team and family in the district. The visibility of our leaders is essential. Being in classrooms, having conversations with students and teachers, and establishing a constant encouraging presence are what

> we are striving to do. As leaders, we have to demonstrate our passion, spirit, and positivity as cornerstones to building trust and confidence. We want to have a prevailing culture of positivity. We want our schools to establish a presence of welcoming. We are trying to create a vibe, a sense of wanting to know students, and passion and belief in each other.

When the pandemic hit and we had to provide virtual learning, JCPS mobilized and went to work. In April 2020, to augment the devices already in the district, JCPS purchased and distributed another 25,000 laptops to students. This was completed in two weeks! The district mailed the devices to the homes of students as a means to streamline and recognize the struggle for families. The JCPS tech department pulled together and worked with a great sense of urgency and clearly displayed "committed positivity in action."

Kermit Belcher, JCPS's CTO, states: "We knew we needed to step up, and we did, with enthusiasm, and we knew we were making a difference for students and teachers." Another great example of trust and spirit building was exemplified by how JCPS schools connected with students and families in the fall of 2020, when the district was all virtual. Schools conducted drive-by Meet and Greet Your Teacher events. At Norton Elementary School, parents, students, and staff all felt the need for and importance of connecting. Teachers greeted and met students as parents drove through the parking lot. Norton Principal Marcella Minoque observes, "You could see, hear, and feel the students' excitement to meet and see their teachers. We distributed packets that included a laptop and hot spot, as well as other things they might need. It was a joyful time." Parents commented on the well-planned and organized effort and expressed appreciation and thanks to the teachers and the staff.

Pollio talks about how the new culture starts with loving what you are doing. Great teachers love teaching, and great principals love being principals:

> I was a principal here for several years, and when an adult walks up to me to tell me about a conversation we had from when they were students, how it affected their life, it affirms what we are doing. Students want and need teachers and administrators to care about them. When we ask students to tell us about their best teachers, it's always about the teachers' passion and caring. Conversations translate to caring to love for so many.

COLLABORATIVE SCIENCE: INNOVATION AND THE PANDEMIC

If you want to change the culture of a system, you need inspiring goals and themes *and* concrete elements that exemplify the new direction in action. A quick aside about our change theory: the nuance requires steps that are *specific but not imposed.* Of the three core principles—positive climate, racial equity, and Backpack of Skills—the most concrete one was the Backpack. This innovation has major implications for the future of pedagogy (goals and means of learning), and related assessment of outcomes. It warrants some detail here.

While many of the ideas that have become a central part of the new curriculum at JCPS preceded the pandemic, it was the experience of the latter that became the deep catalyst for deeper change. Pollio describes the breakthrough situation in the following words:

> I had heard educators talk tirelessly over the past 10 months [covering much of 2020] that "we cannot go back to the way things were pre-COVID-19." We kept saying the system had to change, but nothing was happening. So I said, "We have been saying that the system had to change, but *what* exactly are we talking about? If we're not intentional about it when we get back to opening schools, we are going to be right back to the way things were."

> So we put together a task force that was responsible for figuring out a collective plan. I said that I was not going to dictate what should happen, but that I was going to light the kindling so we can have the task force recommend the changes to focus on.

Need we note the science of collaboration at work here? Urgency and direction combined with joint determination—nuanced leadership at its best.

Superintendent Pollio had written his doctoral dissertation on the topic of standards and grading practices and considers it one of the most detrimental components of the K–12 system. "It's a matter of racial equity," he says. JCPS was already shifting to a new system of designing assessment and learning when COVID-19 hit. The system made structural changes, like establishing the start time at 9 a.m. in the new virtual model instead of at 8 a.m. or earlier. Many kids thrived with the later start time, Pollio noted.

Urgency and direction combined with joint determination—nuanced leadership at its best.

The task force itself took the opportunity to focus on new proficiency standards. Again, from Pollio: "There is nothing that hurts kids and disengages them more than the traditional curriculum." Interestingly, this is a conclusion that Fullan arrived at and spelled out as academic obsession, a wrong driver (Fullan, 2021; we will take this up more generally again in the final chapter). "I am a huge fan of the new deep learning," says Pollio as the system moved to practices where students could pursue authentic learning that inspire and enable them to learn more in depth. We note here the overlap with the deep learning work being done in the New

Pedagogies for Deep Learning initiative in several countries, including the United States (Fullan et al., 2018; Quinn et al., 2020).

The Backpack of Five Skills, arising from the task force, was the mechanism that framed the new learning:

1. Persistence and resilience
2. Communication
3. Collaboration
4. Innovation
5. Globally and culturally competent citizens

The Backpack of Success Skills is a digital platform requiring students to use their life and learning experiences to enhance their understanding of math and literacy, preparing them to be good communicators, problem solvers, and collaborators. As Pollio says,

> We believe that each student needs a Backpack of Skills, success skills—and that means life skills. Academics are important, but we are also focused on the other skill sets related to life functions: being able to communicate and carry on conversations, knowing how to collaborate and how to work with others, and how to solve problems and innovate.

Pollio believes that all students and staff need a true sense of belonging:

> We know the beliefs, attitudes, and actions of adults in schools have a huge impact on student success.
>
> We are developing deeper engagements in classrooms. We have students collect examples of their work and create digital

> portfolios. We ask students to defend their readiness to move forward in Grades 5, 8, and 12. We know content knowledge is important, but knowing how to communicate and demonstrating resilience is also vital. We balance formal protocols for collaboration with latitude and respect for individual context. A comprehensive and well-thought-out instructional design that aligns with new digital and pedagogical foundations is an evolving priority for all instructional leaders. One of the real challenges is for a teacher to move toward a participatory culture where students lead the instruction process by sharing what and how they are learning and what it means to them.

Pollio continues:

> We wanted kids to practice and become proficient. Every kid has a digital Backpack. We want them to take artifacts of learning. If I work with three other kids and we present on a project, we put a video of that work in the pack under the collaboration folder. Throughout their time in school, kids assemble artifacts on specific themes. Then in Grades 5, 8, and 12—the transitional years—all kids present [are formally assessed on] what they have done, presenting to a panel of three or four relevant teachers. In front of the committee, they show what they have done, and provide examples of their artifacts of learning. What this has enabled teachers to do is to authentically assess kids.

The Backpack of Success Skills innovation at JCPS is a powerful example of how the culture of learning has changed. We witnessed several demonstrations of the Backpack method in action (remotely). The traditional way of teaching (knowledge, worksheets, segmented academic subjects, etc.) has been replaced with new learning that we very much recognize as *deep learning.* Students work individually and in small groups, guided by teachers. They pursue small projects guided by key themes and questions. During the pandemic, JCPS staff organized and implemented after-school virtual club offerings for all students—everything from building blocks, art, music, games, and puzzles for fun and time to connect with other students. The response was immediate, and students and parents offered praise and appreciation. "For us kids, this a big deal. We really, really miss seeing each other and talking and stuff. We are meeting other kids who have some similar interests, and this is fun and important," a fifth-grade student shared.

LOOKING AHEAD

The Backpack method had teachers working individually and with peers to understand mutually what was being learned and how it was being taught. The culture was powerful, transparent, and specific. Trust and accountability went hand in hand. In this very large district, teachers' collaboration within and across schools—*professional capital,* as Andy Hargreaves and Fullan called it—increased dramatically.

In three years, a highly complex, diversified school district with almost 100,000 students went from being a "struggling district," on the verge of being taken over by the state, to an impressive success story. Graduation rates and student success have been on the rise and are improving, although there is much, much work to do. The graduation rate rose four points in the last two years up to 84%. The public supported, with demonstrated enthusiasm, the passage of the largest school bond referendum in Kentucky history in the fall of 2020. Ninety-five percent of students took one or more advanced courses and enrollment in advanced placement (AP) classes has increased. JCPS students earned over $100 million in scholarships. More recently, JCPS students created over half a million artifacts for their virtual backpack portfolios. More than 23,000 students completed their defenses in Grades 5, 8, and 12.

One of the compelling stories of the confluence of collaborative spirit was conveyed by the grandmother of a JCPS student and the story of how they learned together.

> I would sit beside my granddaughter as she was doing her virtual classes, to be there to help and support. After a few

> sessions in math class, I realized I was learning new things right along with my granddaughter. I recognized and understood algebra symbols and realized that, what I hadn't understood before, I now understood. Who would have ever thought I could do a one-step equation! I got so motivated I am going to go back to school and earn my GED. I want to be a positive influence on my granddaughter.

Once again, powerful cultural levers—spirit and collaboration working in combination make a world of difference in a short time to the lives of thousands of students, and their families, and the educators that learn with them.

CONCLUSION

Fullan (2019) concluded that *nuance leaders* have "a loyalty to a better future . . . they see below the surface, enabling them to detect patterns and their consequences for the system" (p. 112). We saw this in Shelby County. Facing immense challenges, this large complex system has become even more proactive about the future by including kindergarten, restructuring some schools, expanding outdoor learning spaces, further developing emotional intelligence, creating theater and visual arts, preparing students to work in the global economy, and more. It is their strong commitment to spirit work and deep collaboration that gives them the drive and confidence to tackle and help create a better future. They are not doing this despite the complexity, but rather *because* new challenges present new opportunities to innovate.

The Jefferson County case contains two powerful lessons. First, with focused leadership, a core inspiring agenda, and persistent involvement of those at all levels, you can transform a large organization. Second, Jefferson County has made outstanding progress in a relatively short period—less than three years. Spirit and collaboration accelerate momentum in mutually reinforcing ways.

6 WEST COAST DISTRICTS (UNITED STATES) IN ACTION

As we swing west, we have three districts to consider: San Ramon Valley in California, Highline School District in the greater Seattle area, and Chula Vista in Southern California near the Mexican border.

Dr. John Malloy

SAN RAMON VALLEY UNIFIED SCHOOL DISTRICT (CALIFORNIA)

ANTICIPATING THE FUTURE

Relationships are all there is. Everything in the universe only exists because it is in relationship to everything else. Nothing exists in isolation.

—*Turning to One Another* (Wheatley, 2009)

As a new superintendent to San Ramon Valley, Dr. John Malloy was just finishing his first year when we studied the district. He had moved, so to speak, from the ridiculous to the sublime. Malloy had spent most of his career in Ontario, Canada. In fact, Fullan had studied Malloy as he became director (superintendent) of the mammoth Toronto District School Board in Toronto (TDSB) in January 2016 through his term until his departure in May 2020. The Toronto case study is featured in Fullan's book, *Nuance* (2019). TDSB, with almost 600 schools and 250,000 students, is the eighth-largest school district in North America. Let's just say that Malloy found a way to have regular relationships with his 28 "families of schools" by revamping the system to have 28 area superintendents overseeing 20 or so schools each (see Fullan, 2019, pp. 50–61). In May 2020, Malloy resigned near the end of his contract, and in the summer of 2020 became superintendent of San Ramon Valley Unified School District (SRVUSD) in the East Bay region of San Francisco. With 36 schools and 32,000 students, it is barely larger than one of the 28 areas in TDSB.

In the summer of 2020, Malloy did not hit the ground running; he hit the ground in a full-on sprint. He and the SRVUSD leadership team worked with constant urgency and purpose to prepare for school during the pandemic. Malloy is a people person, and he invested his time, energy, and spirit in building relationships with teachers, principals, parents, students, and community members. Malloy's deep commitment to every student shines through when he talks about the district: "Our collective urgency to support our teachers and students defines who we are."

The San Ramon Valley Unified School District is located 30 miles east of San Francisco. As we noted above, it comprises 36 schools, serving over 32,000 students. SRVUSD is one of the top-performing districts in California. Over 94% of graduates attend college or university and over 98% graduate from high school. SRVUSD schools have received numerous awards, including the coveted State Department of Education's Distinguished Schools Award over 50 times. Community and parental support are well established with county parent-teacher association (PTA) membership of over 20,000 and the San Ramon Valley Education Foundation offers significant support in a variety of ways. The district is proud of its accomplishments but is committed to improving. The district is focusing on equity and the well-being of all students. The interesting question is *What does a high-flying district do for its next act?*

Equally interesting is *What does Malloy do in such a radically different context than he was used to?* Malloy was named the 2018 Canadian Superintendent of the Year and he is recognized in Canada and the United States as an exemplary leader. He is a fierce advocate for all students and believes all teachers need to see and feel support and service from the district. Malloy has focused work on the importance of collaboration and engagement as part of the instructional model. He has demonstrated consistent leadership in building trusting relationships and is not reluctant to challenge bias.

Prior to his work with the Toronto School Board, Malloy served as one of the assistant deputy ministers of education at the Ontario Ministry of Education and as superintendent of the Hamilton-Wentworth District School Board (west of Toronto). During his career, he has served as a teacher, counselor, assistant principal, and principal. He is the author of numerous articles and is in demand as a speaker and presenter. Malloy leads with his heart and is working on building deep spirit in SRVUSD.

We need to think of the San Ramon Valley case differently because

- It is very high performing in academic terms.
- The board hired a high-profile, innovative new superintendent in Malloy, possibly because they sensed that some changes were needed given an unknown future.
- Malloy has only known the district in COVID-19 times, having arrived at lockdown, and, as we write this chapter, just completing his first full year before California schools return to in-classroom schooling.

As authors, we are flirting with the future in this case, as everything is about to happen in real time. Once again, the pandemic comes along at exactly the right time to be a catalyst for change: a high-performing system in traditional terms is virtually (no pun intended) offered the opportunity to reconsider its future.

In the following section, we start with getting to know Malloy and the system, but the most interesting issue is how can a new superintendent and district do this while producing a strategic plan in short order (a year) under conditions of chaos. Since this is a case of planning to act but not yet having the opportunity to do so, we ask the reader to view the plan that they did produce (which we share below) in terms of its clarity, inspiration, and potential.

NEW SPIRIT AND CARING TO CONVICTION

When we interviewed Malloy, we found what we expected: someone who was simultaneously addressing the immediate crisis while interacting with all groups to begin considering the next phase. The board required Malloy to lead the process to develop the next five-year strategic plan. Malloy told the board, and us in an interview, that he did not like "to plan to plan," so he proposed that he would consult widely to produce a plan that would enable the district to hit the ground running in the fall of 2021. And this is what he and they did.

Malloy is not the least bit hesitant to share his belief on what is the key to building trust and spirit in schools:

> The most important piece is that we all have to belong, that our voice matters. We have to know each other's truth, and then we have to be fully committed to mutual respect. The foundation of well-being is equity. We have a real role to play as leaders . . . we must provide clear directions and then provide constant nurturance that binds us together. The path to our improvement is based on building a learning community of trust. A strong cultural foundation is essential for success in any district. It starts with defining beliefs and daily practices, like holding high expectations for all students, treating everyone with kindness and respect, understanding that when adults share and work well together students are watching and learning, embracing personal accountability, and creating a tenacious disposition as a team of learners.

"We have to know each other's truth, and then we have to be fully committed to mutual respect. The foundation of well-being is equity." —**Dr. John Malloy**

SRVUSD leaders understand, with Malloy leading the way,

> That you have to expect to happen what you want to happen. We have to establish that we have a job to do, and we will not settle for less. As we work on developing pervasive efficacy, we are building momentum. We should be able to see the difference, feel the difference, and achieve different and better results when we are learning together.

As noted in *Leading With Soul,* "The heart of leadership is in the hearts of leaders. You have to lead from something deep in your heart" (Bolman & Deal, 2011). Malloy shares that he has some reticence to talk directly of love but believes that consistent and insistent caring for each other is an absolute priority. Malloy elaborates:

> We have to be intentional about creating and sustaining conversations in our classrooms. We establish agreed-upon norms that guide our structure. Learning to listen is key for instructional dialogue to occur. We need to develop learning communities that are the right size to engage in conversation so that students develop the confidence and the capacity to engage in educational dialogue. Students have to learn the strategies and have the tools to be active members and to have a voice. They learn that everyone has a voice in the learning and that their voice matters. It is so important to understand that this is a priority and that time, effort, and reflection are needed in order for students to develop the ability to be conversant.

We also found snippets of these values as people referred to some examples of what went on during the past 18 months. SRVUSD District Administrator Jon Campopiano underscores the serious effort to make sure students have a voice:

> In the fall of 2020, at the height of the pandemic, SRVUSD selected its first student school board member and established a districtwide student senate. This work formalized the effort to make sure we are using student voices, innovation, and creativity to solve problems and plan for the future. Student leaders have risen to the work and offer thoughtful input and ask hard questions. The heart and spirit of the student voice have inspired us all.

Another example comes Sara Clancey, a second-grade teacher at Live Oak Elementary in SRVUSD:

> A few years ago, I was working with a student with significant emotional issues. It didn't take much to set him off and he would turn over desks, throw books and papers, and yell and cry. One time I saw that he was about to lose it, and

> I went over and kneeled beside his desk and softly asked him what was wrong. At first, he started yelling, but I asked again, even softer, and then he calmed down and explained why he was upset. This was significant for me and it was a learning point for me. Kindness, love, caring, and listening were the keys to the success with this student. As I reflected on working with this student, I clearly understood that relationships would and should always be a priority.

And a third example, from Courtney Konopackey at Stone Middle School:

> A few years ago, I had a student who, at the beginning of the year, would not make eye contact with anyone, did not interact with other students, and was in class but not *into* class. One day at the end of class, I asked him about a computer game (I knew he was into games), and we struck up a conversation. He helped me solve a problem I was having, and from that day on we had connected. He started opening up in class a little and interacting with other students. He grew, I grew, and the class grew as we nurtured our relationships.

Malloy models his own values not just for staff but for the community. He has conducted 30 meetings with groups of 10 parents each to help create understanding. "I have to listen. It is important to listen deeply, to understand expectations through questions and then to demonstrate follow-up action as needed," Malloy shared. Instructional design that engages teachers as mentors and coaches for students can make a powerful difference.

When excellence, equity, and well-being develop together, they generate a cadre of caring learners working together. Listen-and-learn is a key leadership quality that we have found in our work. Leaders work to forge unity of purpose over time (see Fullan, 2019). Malloy believes that humor is an important ingredient in the development of school culture and the well-being of students and teachers: "When we laugh together (with respect), it adds a lightness and enhances creativity."

> When excellence, equity, and well-being develop together, they generate a cadre of caring learners working together.

SCIENCE OF COLLABORATION

Malloy states that

> We believe that the definition of *collaboration success* is "We connect at such a level that we are different because of it. We allow ourselves to be vulnerable and realize that we can and will change. When school leaders are willing to give everyone public voice to the information (the content) and then to listen and process them together, the information becomes amplified. It is important to establish real commitment, to strategize and prioritize for collaboration. The key to our improvement is collaboration and learning together . . . none of us can do it alone. When we demonstrate commitment to collaboration, we create a sense of value for each other. When we reflect on how we work together and how we are doing, we grow together. Students need to collaborate to prepare for their future."

Malloy stresses that principals and assistant principals have to play a huge role in the evolution of collaboration:

> As positional leaders, it is incumbent on us to create conditions for the staff to have room and support to grow new skills. Leaders have to show up and model the learning dispositions they want to see. We have to be present and take initiative to build momentum. Although we get terribly distracted by the day-to-day demands of our work, it is important and urgent to focus our attention on the heart of our efforts. We have to be willing to change. We lead by showing our willingness to change. Organizations will always change

> and are never static. We must come with passion and vigor when we come to work. As a wise leader once said, "You can only go one way when you are coasting . . . downhill."

High school principal Megan Keefer knows that the work of building trust is not easy:

> Recently our high school had another experience with hate speech. Our superintendent was swift in his directive to notify the community with total transparency. While the process was painful, we became stronger from it. Instead of the familiar refrain from students that "admin won't do anything," we needed our students to know we could and would do better. We held student forums and expanded collaboration with students to solve problems and build better relationships. Yes, our students were angry and hurt, but when they saw how we responded, they noticed and then became the heart of the response. They responded by recognizing that they would learn from this act of hate by countering it with something bigger and stronger—love.

It is too early to tell how SRVUSD will fare with its new leader. The interesting equation is that the SRVUSD is an award-winning high-performing district that hires a high-performing external superintendent to help them do even better—but when you are highly successful, what is "better"? A third party—COVID-19—joins the fray and forces the matter: *How should we leverage the pandemic experience to renew our future?* The coming period provides a new test, and as we said, a serendipitous, unique opportunity to deepen big spirit and the science of collaboration.

LOOKING AHEAD

SRVUSD did produce its strategic plan, which it approved in June 2021. The plan is reproduced here in Figure 6.1.

The plan is a model of integrating past strengths and future aspirations: academic excellence, the deep learning agenda, and

San Ramon Valley Unified School District Strategic Directions

Built on a foundation of academic excellence, we are broadening our definition of *success*. *Success* means our teams create and nurture:

Equity

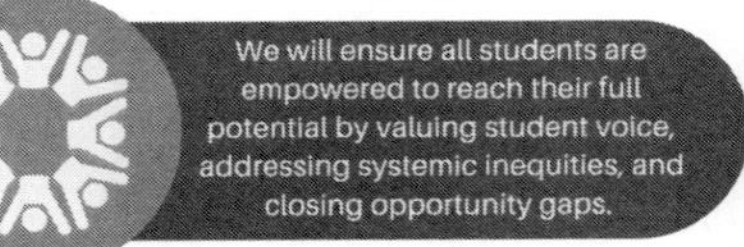

We will ensure all students are empowered to reach their full potential by valuing student voice, addressing systemic inequities, and closing opportunity gaps.

Social Emotional Well-Being

We are committed to creating and nurturing inclusive learning environments where all students, staff, and families feel deeply connected to their school community.

Deep Learning and Innovation

We will create learning environments that empower students to own their learning so they find purpose, meaning, and joy in their education and excel in post-high school endeavors.

Shared Leadership

We will create the conditions for shared leadership by building a culture of trust, collegiality, and shared responsibility with students, staff, and families.

Stewardship of Resources

We will maximize resources including time, talent and finances, to advance our student success goals.

Culture of Responsiveness

We will effectively serve all stakeholders by listening, responding promptly, changing practices when appropriate, and communicating the rationale for decisions so students remain the focus of our efforts.

WWW.SRVUSD.NET

SRVUSD... Dedicated to academic excellence where <u>all</u> students thrive and succeed in innovative and inclusive learning environments.

Success means our students:

- Achieve academically
- Experience social and emotional well-being
- Develop curiosity, confidence and independence as learners
- Appreciate the importance of teams and collaboration
- Demonstrate empathy and compassion
- Determine their purpose and understand the importance of service
- Set and achieve goals
- Love learning

shared destination. Indeed, it exemplifies spirit and collaboration. It presents a strong degree of clarity around the aspirations the system holds. The way in which it honors the work of the past ("built on a foundation of academic excellence") is crystal clear, and it invites staff into broadening the definition of *success* to encompass deep learning. The clarity of language and the attention to practical actions in some of the goal areas will help engage and inspire staff as well. The "culture of responsiveness," for example, is very specific: listening, responding promptly, changing practices, and communicating rationale. These are clear expectations with few places to hide or defend actions that might not be aligned; they are in fact a good foundation for the development of clear standards of practice and expectations going forward to educate students in competencies geared to post-pandemic society.

We will follow this case carefully in the next period to see how it plays out in the post-pandemic era, and in the context of major reform in California in which one of us (Fullan) is involved.

HIGHLINE WASHINGTON SCHOOL DISTRICT

THE HIGHLINE PROMISE

People become good at life when they feel safe, valued, and have a sense of purpose and meaning. There is a need to be engaged in meaningful activities that contribute to the well-being of others.

— *Deep Learning* (Fullan et al., 2018);
The Devil Is in the Details (Fullan & Gallagher, 2020)

Dr. Susan Enfield speaks with passion when she talks about students in the Highline Washington School District. When she says that "we have a commitment that we call the Highline Promise, to know every student by name, strength, and need in the Highline District," she speaks with deep conviction. Enfield has led the district for eight years and has exercised leadership to build a strong foundation of learning and love in this complex district.

The district has established five primary goals to guide the work and daily life of students. First, there's a focus on creating school cultures where students feel welcomed and safe and mutual respect for students and staff is ever present. Second, every student will make a year's worth of growth annually. Third, students will graduate with the problem-solving and critical-thinking skills necessary to live and work responsibly in a digital world. Fourth, students will graduate bilingual and biliterate, and fifth, students will graduate from high school prepared for the future they choose.

Dr. Susan Enfield

Along with the five goals, Highline leaders have identified foundation elements to support each goal for each student. Equity-based practices are a focus so that all students have an equal chance at success and bias is not tolerated. Instructional practices will reduce achievement gaps by using culturally responsive instruction. Relationships will support this promise to students and the need to have open, two-way communication with families. Increasing support of social and emotional needs will increase student success.

It is clear that the district is leading with love and spirit work.

Highline District is in the greater Seattle, Washington, area and is composed of 33 schools, 19,000 students, with 99 languages being spoken. The district has seen a steady increase in the graduation rate for the last seven years and in 2020 was at 84%, a 21% increase since 2013. The district has flourished with Enfield's leadership team, creating conditions for student and teacher success. Although almost 70% of students qualify as students of poverty, the district has been relentless with its work toward success for all students. Enfield has a deep belief in all students that has been a distinguishing hallmark of her leadership. She graduated from the University of California, Berkeley, and received her doctoral degree from Harvard University. Enfield is respected by peers across the United States and was named the recipient of the 2020 AASA Women in Leadership Award. Enfield leads with trust and love, and that model has set the tone for children and staff. She works at being visible and visiting every school and classroom. In turn, she stresses, "we promote leaders who are engaged and understand the focus is on service to schools."

"As part of the Promise, we established a system where every student in the district would be assigned an adult who would check in with them every week to see how they are doing. It was difficult for some who saw the commitment beyond the role of being a teacher, but eventually, everyone bought in," Enfield states. "We incorporated the 'every student an adult' goal into our strategic plan, and it became tied into our Promise."

BUILDING THE SPIRIT

A familiar theme in our eight cases arises early in our discussion with Enfield:

> We begin everything we do with the Highline Promise, that we really know the students and know their strengths and their needs. This is our core value. We have devoted significant time and energy to develop relationships. We build trust by showing our leadership dispositions of giving time. We have to work at knowing each other; we can't take it for granted. We have to know all of our employees, know our families and be consistent. Trust is built on consistency.

Tremain Holloway, principal of Maritime High School, shares how the Highline Promise works for him:

> I truly believe that culture is a feeling and spirit that permeates every class and the entire school. It is a set of expectations and conditions that support all that we do. The Promise is not a strategy but a way of being. Everything we do is centered on

> building relationships with students . . . knowing their names, knowing their strengths and needs, and preparing them for their future. I am humbled to be part of a district where the student perspective comes first and equity is at the core of all we do.

The spirit of Highline is rooted in a deep and relentless belief in every student, along with shared conviction by all employees.

Faith is another aspect of big spirit across our cases. Enfield expresses what *faith* means:

> You own it when you get it wrong. You don't lie. I know some of our children are harmed when we don't get it right. We have to reflect on what we are doing and what is working and what needs some more work. Personal reflection on our experience is how we learn from experience. And, of course, reflecting on practice by observing practice, and by engaging in conversations about our reflections, builds school culture hospitable to both learning and the community. We have to hire and develop the right principals that have that innate sense for trust and love. They have to have "it" in their bones. We can only have trust when we communicate with families, students, and staff. We do "Soup With the Supe" where we meet students and staff and have some soup . . . and just talk informally. We are working on expanding and developing our conversations. We have a lot of work to do. We have had conversations about race and identity, but we still have a long way to go. We believe our instruction should be loaded with conversations.

Another key concept for Enfield is that of conviction:

> We measure conviction by asking students if they believe that their teachers care about them. We survey all students and staff as to their perceptions and if they feel supported. This takes constant effort to build coherence in our collective dispositions. I was visiting a class one time and a fifth-grade student was asleep with her head on the desk. The principal and I talked to her (Eliza) and we (she and I) kind of bonded. I went back later and met with Eliza and we got to know each

> other. She told me that one of her most favorite things was chicken teriyaki, and the next time we met I brought her some and we ate together. During the pandemic, I checked with the principal, and they lost touch with Eliza. We were able to track her down and we went to see her in a pitiful hotel with several people living in one room. We brought the family a gift card and, of course, lots of chicken teriyaki. Eliza was so glad to see us and so happy that we came to see her. Our students must be "truly seen by us, by all of us."

The Highline Promise is supported by all staff with a sense of shared pride and conviction. Mona Plenesi, Highline school resource officer (SRO), conveys her thoughts:

> I truly believe our success in getting through the pandemic was based on work before the pandemic. Highline has worked for years building relationships with students and families and working every day at overcoming obstacles to helping families. Building trust and using positive reinforcement have created a sense of unity with Highline and the communities it serves. We are all fortunate to be part of a district that lives up to its promise.

Susan Enfield, like our other superintendents, finds it natural to talk about love:

> We lead with love with all that we do. We talk about what love looks like for students and how they know it. We agree we show love through our daily actions, it's how we show conviction. If we love our students, we should love our work with students. Our demonstrated joy and having fun are messages about how we love.

"We agree we show love through our daily actions, it's how we show conviction. If we love our students, we should love our work with students. Our demonstrated joy and having fun are messages about how we love." —**Dr. Susan Enfield**

COLLABORATIVE EVOLVEMENT

Once again from Enfield we see that spirit and collaboration must be intertwined:

> We have structures to support inquiry-based instruction where we collaborate as part of the design. We have encouraged and developed our collaboration formally and informally. We have a lot of work to do to grow our competency. Right now we have a lot of hit-and-miss with our collaborative dialogue. We use student teams to advise and guide our thinking. We want students to choose their futures and to know and understand the collaborative skills they will need. We know students like to learn from one another, and we need to promote and amplify our efforts in this area.

Kellie Hernandez, principal of Madrona Elementary School, understands that spirit means growing the capacity of teachers to collaborate effectively.

> As school leaders, we have worked with structured PLCs [professional learning communities] to help us grow together in our efforts to live up to our promise. We have also recognized the need for school leaders to engage in conversations when we can share celebrations but also seek out support and help when needed. We recognize that when we lift each other, we are all lifted.

We also see that spirit and collaboration mutually intensify as they are built into the culture of the district. For Enfield, it requires constant attention: "people-focused leaders." Enfield states that one of the aspects she worries about and works on is leadership stability. She stresses, "You have to work on this all the time. As leadership is crucial, but also demanding, we need constant attention."

Enfield concludes:

> We know that teachers also like to learn from other teachers, and we are mobilizing efforts to leverage more opportunities

> for collegial learning. We learn more about collegiality by practicing and then working on developing the same effort with students. We have equity forums to establish social and emotional guidance and support for bus drivers and all staff. When we say we love our students, it has to be genuine. We have to have people-focused leaders—not outcomes first, people first.

In sum, we see consistent themes in Highline as in the previous six cases. Highline has had a longer period than the others to settle into a pattern around our twin themes. But it is clear that this is a continuous journey.

CHULA VISTA ELEMENTARY SCHOOL DISTRICT (CALIFORNIA)

HARMONY

Modern managers concentrate mostly on the rational side of enterprise. Neglecting the spiritual dimension, they overlook a powerful untapped source of energy and vitality.

—*Leading With Soul* (Bolman & Deal, 2011)

Chula Vista Elementary School District (CVESD) was one of ten positive outlier districts selected for intensive study by Stanford University's Learning Policy Institute (LPI). The positive outlier sample consisted of districts among California's 1,000-plus local jurisdictions that performed measurably above what could have been expected given their demographics (Learning Policy Institute, 2021). These findings were collected prior to the pandemic and validate

Dr. Francisco Escobado

a strong coordinated focused organization with consistent measurable results for its students and community.

LPI organized its findings around four main themes:

1. Interdependence with respect to philosophy and structure (clear decision-making process amid decentralized operations)
2. The building of a learning organization (through educator and leader development)
3. Incremental and deliberate implementation of core priorities
4. Support and interventions for target subgroups (keen analytic focused on student subgroups)

The LPI study quotes Dr. Francisco Escobedo referencing a time near the beginning of his tenure as superintendent, specifically about the district's longstanding system of decentralized decision making:

> I think part of it [lack of clarity and cohesion] was the work in isolation that I saw schools work under and how certain principals floundered, especially the new ones—the lack of support and connection they had in a district as large as ours. The principal turnover was pretty great because of that. I just said, "We need to retain our leaders. We also need to create a better support structure for our teachers." (Learning Policy Institute, 2021, p. 9)

Assistant Superintendent Dr. Gloria Ciriza put the goal this way:

> We knew that in a system as big as ours, it was going to be really important to build instructional leadership capacity at each one of our school sites. To do that, the professional learning sessions were designed so that principals and/or key teacher leaders from each cohort were the facilitators. We understood how essential it was for principals and teacher leaders to learn the material together and then collaborate and plan for ways to take the new learning back to their school. (Learning Policy Institute, 2021, p. 27)

In our own study, we started with Superintendent Escobedo. He smiles when he talks about students in the Chula Vista Elementary School District: "Our students face so many challenges and yet they come to our schools with so much heart and enthusiasm. They know we care deeply for them and are determined to help every student be successful." For more than a decade, the superintendent has led the district with distinct attention to creating a loving and nurturing environment. Each morning in every school, teachers greet each student with a handshake and smile as they enter their classroom. The district has embraced a continuous improvement philosophy with the foundational belief that everyone can grow, learn, and improve every day.

The Chula Vista Elementary School District is located between the city of San Diego and the United States and Mexico border and serves almost 30,000 students in 46 schools. It is the largest elementary district in California. CVESD embraces the belief that "each child is an individual with great worth." More than two-thirds of the students are Latino/Latina, 87% are nonwhite, over half come from low-income families, and more than a third are English language learners (ELLs). Despite the challenges, the district performance ranks among the highest in the county. The district has focused on the whole child and on innovative programs and services to meet the needs of students. The district and individuals have received numerous recognitions honoring student achievement, visual and performing arts, and positive school climates.

CVESD's improved academic outcomes are part of a larger story where a culture of trust has been established among staff, students, and all employees. This work has taken years and requires constant attention. It has become a central feature of a well-established spirit of the district, the students, and the staff.

Escobedo started a career in public service as a police officer in San Diego. "I interacted with students and families and knew I could do more, so I decided to become an educator and never looked back." Since 2010, he has served as CVESD's superintendent. Escobedo has been an active civic leader in the community, serving as past president of the Chamber of Commerce and in numerous other leadership roles. He has initiated healthy student and wellness efforts and he has been a leader in the effort to preserve music in schools and, as a result, has received national recognition with the AASA Fine Arts Leadership Award. Escobedo leads with a distinct kindness and sensitivity toward others. He received his undergraduate degree from Yale University and earned his doctoral degree from the University of California. His calm and determined presence as a leader has been instrumental in a sense of hope and spirit in the district.

LIFTING SPIRITS

Escobedo talks about the spiritual side of his leadership:

> Building trust is complex and it is fragile, but it is the foundation of our relationships and our ability to meet the needs of our students. We lead with love and care for all of our students and are firm in our understanding that how we treat students is the first and most important message they receive from us. Our leadership team—central office, principals, and myself—works on being visible as part of our efforts to establish trust. We encourage constant conversations about our work and what our goals are.

As Margaret Wheatley says, "When a community of people discovers that they share a concern, change begins. There is no power equal to a community discovering what it cares about. Real change begins with the simple act of people talking about what they care about" (Wheatley, 2009).

> "We measure conviction by asking students if they believe their teachers care about them. We acknowledge how important it is to show our students and each other love through our daily actions." —**Dr. Francisco Escobedo**

An excellent example of how strong spirit has evolved and connected school staff to lift and support all families is shared by Angelica Maldonado, who serves as a CVESD district parent engagement liaison:

> After I had given a presentation on our family resource centers, sponsored by the Chula Vista Community Collaborative, to our preschool teachers, one of the teachers reached out to me. She shared with me that a Japanese family with two preschoolers with special needs had just lost the father of the family to cancer. They had no support system or mastery of the English language. One of our ELL Japanese teachers asked that we mobilize our resources to help this family. We did just that. We provided a variety of services, including a translator, food, and guidance related to any needs. The district, school, and community services worked to lift this family and are providing ongoing support.

Maldonado continues,

> We position and focus our central office on supporting, coaching, and encouraging and affirming good work. Equally important is making recommendations for improvement and growth. We survey all teachers and students to gain insight into their perceptions and if they feel supported. It is important that students and families encounter like-minded supportive leaders in many aspects of the district's work.

Depree called this phenomenon "roving leaders" in *Leadership Is an Art*: "Roving leaders are those indispensable people in our lives who are there when we need them. Roving leaders model the way forward" (Depree, 2004).

Escobedo talks about deepening the spirit and conviction of Chula Vista's culture that focuses on students and encompasses all adults in the community:

> We measure conviction by asking students if they believe their teachers care about them. As part of our system of professional development, we have had deep reflective conversations about our collective empathy and how we can develop that in every teacher. Faith is born out of consistency and is the soul of our

> organization. We acknowledge how important it is to show our students and each other love through our daily actions.

Escobedo shares a personal story about his experience.

> I had been working with a student, Angel, and he was struggling and would have little fits. I started spending some time with him, mainly letting him know that we care about him—you know students need to hear this every day—and that we believe in him. A couple of years later, I saw him at a public event—he had moved to another district—and he came running up to me and was so excited to share with me that he was doing well. He told me he was still on the right path. His smile was so bright, and my smile mirrored his. We knew we cared about each other.

One of the most striking features of Chula Vista is how they have developed a comprehensive partnership with all social sector agencies in the broader community. The district has explicit formal and informal relationships with the county, the public health department, the city, and various health providers. Chula Vista places great emphasis on wellness.

Most remarkable is that every member of the cabinet (the senior team of ten or so) is expected (and paid by the school board) to join the board of a local community organization. Superintendent Escobedo is a board member of the YMCA, another member is on the board of a hospital consortium, and a third is in the Chamber of Commerce. This was by design, states Escobedo. "In the contracts of my cabinet members, I wrote down that a certain amount of money was earmarked to be part of a community organization."

Within the district, Chula Vista has five family resource centers supporting 46 schools. It is, explains Escobedo, like a one-stop shopping center: parents come if they need food, a place to go, information about how their child can receive certain services, and so on.

All of this existed prior to the pandemic. It was needed back then and is essential many times over now. "I know the power players in our community," says Escobedo. "We have been able to leverage our relationships during the pandemic to ensure that we have resources." COVID-19 has had a devastating impact on this high-poverty largely Latinx community. Chula Vista had the highest infection rate in the state. Many families living in crowded circumstances experienced death directly when grandparents and others died of COVID-19. People in poverty lost jobs and many families moved out of the county, including returning south of the border. There are many homeless students and foster children who easily get lost in the shuffle.

Mental health, wellness, and social-emotional learning (SEL) have become priorities with SEL and emotional intelligence (EQ) sessions being held daily. As we have seen everywhere during the pandemic, explicit connections with families and communities have been on the rise, with one of the positive fallout developments being the likelihood that parent and community relationships will become a permanent feature of school operations and development. Chula Vista is ahead of the game in this domain. Although perhaps a small thing, the superintendent already has a parent cabinet group that meets with him monthly to address ongoing issues. Look for family and community partnerships to be even more strengthened to even deeper levels in the post-pandemic era. What we have called "spirit work" will become all the stronger and more pervasive.

COLLABORATION EXPLORATION

Clearly focused and culture-based collaboration is a core feature of Chula Vista's evolution. Escobedo describes their approach to learning:

> We focus on understanding how students learn, the transmission of information and then the application of that information. We talk about what we see and what we hear from listening to students. We have come to understand and believe that building connections between students is important instructional work. As teachers move from a didactic framework to become facilitators and collaborators, they will need support, direction, and nurturance. Building collaborative

> expertise among students and teachers is central to deeper learning. Developing the capacity to collaborate requires intentional support of sharing, listening, and reflecting together.
>
> Taking the time to communicate means that we understand that students' voices are essential for good teaching and learning. We have worked on developing collective patience as we build our capacity to listen and learn from students. When students have choices and are allowed to control major aspects of their learning, they are more likely to achieve self-motivation for thinking and learning.

Escobedo describes the district's daily preoccupation with relationships to students and their learning:

> We have created morning discussions in the district where we "empty the cup," or get stuff out that needs discussing. We model that in all our meetings, time to put things on the table and work through it, time to figure it out as a team or family. We simply believe that learning together makes a lot of sense for students and staff. We have to work on our leaders' capacity to listen to teachers and students. We must model the behaviors we are trying to inculcate in the district.

CVES district leader Matthew Tessier shares a story about connecting spirit and collaboration:

> I remember a time I was at one of our meeting events and a young girl shared with me that she would like to be a police officer, but sadly said she couldn't because only boys could be police officers. When I heard this, my heart sank, but then I thought about our partnership with the Chula Vista Police Department and several female officers who serve as school resource officers in the community. I got in touch with a female SRO who then visited the little girl in her class on a special visit and shared with her that she could be a police officer just like her.

Connecting as a community collaborative team is one of the strong capacities that Chula Vista has developed, and it is a sure indicator of spirit teamwork.

Recall that "building a learning organization" was one of four core qualities identified by the Learning Policy Institute in their study of positive outliers. It is clear that the Chula Vista system is devoted to helping everyone become learners and leaders, including students, parents, teachers, and all personnel. What we like about the approach is that the system combines specificity with individual and group choice. For example, in their partnership with San Diego State University, Chula Vista jointly worked out a "teacher leadership credential" that is not based on generic ideas but is customized to the Chula Vista culture, which itself is based on common themes and local school customization.

In systems of trust, people are free to create the relationships they need. Trust enables the system to open. More conversations and more diverse and diverging views become important. People decide to work together (Wheatley, 1998).

With the twin foundations of spirit and learning, Francesco Escobedo and the district's educators, in partnership with the larger community, have established a deep culture of success. Due to the disruptions of COVID-19, the next phase for Chula Vista will be another chapter all together, not just a linear extension of what the district has been doing. Another twist: Just as we were finishing our study, Escobedo resigned to take a new position in September 2021 as executive director of the National Center for Urban School Transformation at San Diego State University. Perhaps this presents an opportunity to extend spirit and collaboration from a larger platform vantage point.

CONCLUSION

The possibility of superintendent turnover, of course, applies to all eight of our cases.

In Chapter 7, we take up the main implications of our study, recognizing that we are in the midst of one of the most complex and challenging periods facing society and education in this past century.

PART III

THE FUTURE OF SPIRIT AND COLLABORATION WORK

7 A NEW TOMORROW

Our main message is the realization that both spirit and collaboration are critical; they are both deep concepts (you can't fake either), and they are core human qualities that feed closely on each other to the point that you might as well think of them as fused. The second pair of variables is more personal to you as a leader. What is the nature of the *context* you find yourself in—is it troubled, desirous of change, contains good leaders, stagnant, on the move, etc.? The second factor related to you as a leader is what stage are you at in terms of tenure: beginning, middle, or toward the end of your term? Read our book and each case as they relate to your own situation. Think about your stage of tenure and the nature of the context. Use our core concepts—spirit and collaboration—wisely.

By now we think the reader should be 50% worried and 50% hopeful. When we look at the case for spirit work and the science of collaboration, we hope and believe school leaders will find significant motivation and a sense of urgency as well. But the big question is, *How can we best think about where to go from here?* We will give you three lines of thought: First, how worried should you be, and what are the issues? Second, how can we think and act about the future? Third, what is the role and responsibility of society when it comes to learning?

Our first point is not that we need a replica version of the examples of the cases we have presented. They are U.S.-centric because that was our sample base. More important, they represent cases in a system (worldwide, really) that is in the throes of upheaval and therefore precarious. By the end of this decade, it could go either way: the extinction of humanity as we know it, or the rise and evidence of a new future based on what we call the human paradigm. Let's start first with the "worry list."

THE WORRY LIST

We start with an ad hoc list of items that cut across our cases. They are key agenda items. They are not intended to be a complete list but definitely feature in our cases. We can only highlight them here.

1. Purpose
2. Leadership
3. Equity
4. Well-being
5. Assessment
6. Technology
7. Community
8. Students

First, all the data we can find show that the educational system we have had for almost 200 years no longer has an appealing sense of purpose. The majority of students (we do mean some 70%) are bored or alienated. Getting good grades is no longer an intrinsic motivator. The role of education in society is no longer clear. The labor force is in flux because jobs and life are not predictable.

Second, we need new leadership at all levels, and we will take this up as we go, especially around the crucial learning/change agent role of the young. One could make the obvious point that we need leaders such as the eight in our sample, but remember, this is the worry list. Of course, we need such leaders, but how sustainable is this? One positive aspect that we did not study was the role of mentorship and thus of leadership. We personally know the mentors of many of the eight, and this aspect is an important part of what made these leaders as strong as they have become. But even for these super-charged leaders, how sustainable is it? What toll is the daily churn taking? We did not ask, for example, how many of these leaders faced death threats to themselves or their families (tensions have been high for all the reasons we noted, and superintendents, especially those who are active, can draw the wrong kind of attention). More generally, what has been the resignation or early retirement rate for incumbent superintendents in the past three years? (Try 30%+.) Our point: leading districts in the United States in this decade is not sustainable for incumbents or newcomers. To anticipate a crucial conclusion we make at the end of this chapter, what is essential is to *change the system,* which superintendents do not control.

Third, for more than 40 years, the United States has poured massive money into addressing equity. If anything, the situation has steadily worsened. It is not sufficient (but nonetheless good to do) to help individuals, as our districts did, but again, system change is needed. Our methods of addressing equity have not kept up with increasing diversity. It is likely that everyone in America could be classified as a minority soon. The biases of racism, sexism, and classism now negatively affect the majority of the population.

Fourth, well-being has become all the rage, if you will excuse the pun. The pandemic has hindered and potentially helped—hindered by ravaging the poor and otherwise vulnerable; helped because it has now become a do-or-die matter for large numbers (literally societal decay).

The biases of racism, sexism, and classism now negatively affect the majority of the population.

Fifth, assessment, especially standardized tests, from the start has been the tail that wagged the dog. Our case examples have blunted, but not eliminated, its negative effects. Again, we need to change the system—and in the concluding section, we will see that help may be on the way.

Sixth, technology is now truly ubiquitous. It is interesting that nearly all our eight superintendents (and co-author Mark Edwards) were early advocates of 1-1 computers until they discovered that culture (and spirit) is the driver with technology being the accelerator. But in these pandemic and post-pandemic days, it is harder to figure out and/or control the presence of "digital everything."

Seventh, another two-edged development concerns how the pandemic has highlighted the difficulties of parents and communities. Opportunities, yes, but more overload for schools. More complexities for teachers and parents caught in the closed-open schools' revolving door.

Finally, the plight of students has been further exposed. They are no longer passive recipients of knowledge, but what is their new role? We have some good news in the final section of the chapter.

All in all, the status quo is neither physically nor socially sustainable. The doomsday scenario is now imaginable in real terms and has become the "adjacent possible," to use a term from chaos theory.

In short, the world is hurting, the United States is hurting, and help is needed. Children who are hurting simply have a much harder time learning and surviving. Teachers, parents, principals, administrators, trustees, and all school staff feel the weight of things becoming harsher and more difficult to navigate. Looking at the immediate need for some kind of institutional nurturance, and compounding that with the reality that what we have been doing is stale and doesn't work, should give us two major guideposts. Refocus on getting ready for life, instead of getting ready for a test! Second, another resounding stimulus for action is that we know more. Former Hewlett-Packard (HP) chief executive officer Lewis Platt once famously said, "If HP knew what HP knows, we'd be three times more productive." That's how we feel about our case examples and the other learning that we have been involved in. If leaders only knew what people in the system know, we'd be several times more successful. It is time to mobilize what we know.

COULD IT BE ALMOST TOMORROW?

Getting started takes leadership. Superintendents, principals, teachers, parents, students, school boards, and community leaders will need to lead together (incidentally, we have not taken up school board–superintendent relationships, but the message is the same; see Campbell & Fullan, 2019). None of this is easy. It is very hard, but each of our case districts has started from different places and is progressing at different rates. All are constructing spirit and growing their science of collaboration.

In each of our district cases, the respective superintendents were willing and ready to stand up and lead in a big way. All have different styles and approaches, but all have in common the courage and conviction to know that change is needed and that the journey will be a long one. And they all know in their hearts and heads that this is the right thing to do. Deep and sustained dialogue with principals and teachers that provides time to engage and grow the understanding of first *why*, and then the evolutional embrace of *how*, will establish the first steps of coherence and mutual trust. When you boil it down, the best way to get up to speed is to do the same thing that should be done with students. Work on it every day; talk about how the learning is going and what is needed. Students are messengers to teachers and administrators about the future they are trying to get to. Indeed, students make the best change agents.

Treating everyone—all students, parents, teachers, employees—with respect and honor can be the first and maybe the most vital step of creating deep spirit work. One of the challenges is to understand that working on things like love, respect, and building trust takes daily focus and attention. In our districts, these elements get built in over time. They become embedded into the culture of becoming—"just how we treat each other." Shelby County jumped into a major collaborative effort through the design work for their huge digital implementation. Using a community of leaders to engage, debate, and thrash out a plan worked well. Superintendent Joris Ray noted, "It got noisy sometimes and messy sometimes, but we came together and focused on the students, and we were successful."

It doesn't take long to see students respond to nurturance. When Edwards was a principal, he always took note that students really like to know that you know them by name. Every student should hear an adult call their name, smile when they see them, and know them. It doesn't just happen by chance: it takes work and focus. As San Ramon Valley Unified School District Superintendent John Malloy said earlier, "It is everything to be known." Highline School District has created their *promise* to know each student and to really know them; to know each student is finding and developing the *promise* of each student! Teachers need constant nurturance and encouragement, just like students, and principals must model spirit to students when they make sure teachers are thanked and appreciated. It is important to embrace a philosophy that "we will keep growing and learning . . . forever." One of the most important developmental dispositions to embrace is that this is a journey. We will hit bumps and barriers, we will get tired and exasperated, but we will build our collective endurance and mutual nurturance for us to carry on with gusto! Luvelle Brown has been working for ten years with the Ithaca team to build a loving and caring environment and said it best: "Our work of building and developing loving classrooms and schools goes on every day!"

We can see by each case study that local nuance is a huge factor and being aware of this matters a lot. Each district found leaders emerging in different places who became lead learners and shared their learning to build momentum. Dedicating significant effort (short- and long-term) to professional growth and development is an essential ingredient. Providing structured focus for professional development strategy, linked to building spirit through daily practice, will be needed as well as an array of professional learning efforts. Teachers that are honored by learning with respect and support are likely to learn more. A locally nuanced plan for development that is created in a collaborative environment and is both organic and foundational will enhance and should sustain the long journey. The design and attention for adult learning must be a priority. Utilizing collaborative design and organic nuance drives the effort, and connecting that with energized and ubiquitous local leaders is a dynamic combination. Aaron Spence and Virginia Beach City Schools have worked for years with focused effort on their science of collaboration: "It's who we are and what we do."

Structured listening is a big part of the science of collaboration. Students who practice listening and learn from it are gaining a huge life skill.

Moving from a test focus to a competency focus and from surface learning to deep learning sets the foundation. Student success (learning) and teacher success (learning with students) are the goals. Connecting pedagogy (collaborative and inquiry based) to how students see their future will provide a relevant hook in a big way. The Jefferson County students understand that the Backpack for Life program is way more important than a test. It's about them, it's about their future, and what they will need. Structured listening is a big part of the science of collaboration. Students who practice listening and learn from it are gaining a huge life skill. Teachers who learn to listen to students, and, even more important, are there for each student, create the conditions of effective collaboration and equity. Get rid of the desks or move them together and buy tables (you can save a lot of money). Teachers will evolve into roaming conductors engaging where needed and then working with individuals or small groups or engaging the whole class.

Collaborative dialogue will provide students with unlimited opportunities to learn from the people they learn best from (their peers). This doesn't just happen; the conductor/teacher may breeze in and nudge this way or that, but students learn from daily practice and daily nurturance. Talking about respecting every voice, being patient with each other, and how they learn best together is the life language of equity. This year Edwards's wife taught virtual classes from home. "Over time," he says, "I heard enough to see her students evolve in their ability to discuss things, and listen to each other, and, so important, they became advocates for each other. This didn't just happen; queuing, counseling, and consistency were skills my wife used every day with a ton of nurturance." We heard of examples in each of our case districts where the evolution of collaboration was up and running.

Teachers who develop the capacity of students to be conversant and to listen for purpose are providing the relevance-forward skills that students innately know will be of value. Students working on projects together are commonplace in schools with collaborative design. It is imperative to understand that project work takes planning, design, and collaborative dialogue for the project work to even begin. The energy of students building something together is highly motivational. A few years ago, Edwards was visiting a school in Vancouver, Canada, and the fifth-grade team had developed plans for each class in the school to be the "culture leaders" of the school for a day. One of the classes had students posted throughout the school to greet other students and smile. Edwards asked if it was working, and one little boy smiled at him and said softly "Yes, yes, it is." Edwards smiled too. Sometimes it is the little things.

SYSTEM CHANGE: IT IS TIME FOR SOCIETY TO HELP

It is beyond the scope of this book to start into the system implications of our study, but as we work on the bigger agenda, a link to system change is timely and essential. Fullan and other colleagues around the world are increasingly focusing on whole system success because there is now an urgent need for system change. At the same time, there seems to be greater openness among some policy makers to consider fundamental system transformation. We need policy makers to join the right agenda with a partnership mindset: governors, state commissioners, the President and Federal Secretary of Education, and local politicians. Their stance must be, *What have I got to learn, and what can I do?*

As we were writing this chapter, relevant books from two of our close colleagues arrived on Fullan's doorstep. One was authored by Frederick Hess and Pedro Noguera (2021)—the former arguing from the right, the latter from the left. Using a dialogical mode, they addressed all the themes familiar to our spirit-collaboration cases and then some: the purpose of schooling, school choice, the achievement gap, testing and accountability, socio-emotional learning, civics education, for-profits and privatization, philanthropy, diversity and equity, teacher pay, and COVID-19. They looked for and found some common themes despite their initial differences. Their book is called *A Search for Common Ground.*

Similarly, Dennis Shirley and Andy Hargreaves (2021) offered *Five Paths of Student Engagement,* including Chapter 5's "Standardized Testing: The Archenemy of Engagement." Their five pathways from the learner perspective were intrinsic value, importance, association, empowerment, and mastery—all compatible with spirit work and the science of collaboration. What Shirley and Hargreaves don't address is the question of the day-to-day action strategies for increasing engagement—which, of course, is the forte of our eight cases.

We are getting better formulations of directional solutions and seeming openness on the part of some at the policy level to entertain fundamentally different ideas. These signals prompted Fullan (2021) to formulate a set of four policy drivers for whole system success published in February 2021. The main model is presented in Figure 7.1. It is not a blueprint for transformation, but rather a treasure map to make the set of four drivers the force for major change in learning.

The four right drivers are well-being and learning, social intelligence, equality investment (new monetary investment), and systemness. They are counterforces to the current dominance of wrong or insufficient drivers: academic obsession, machine (artificial) intelligence, austerity (economic policies that grossly favor the rich), and fragmentation (neglect of system policies that help develop systems for the development of all).

7.1 The Right Drivers for Whole System Success

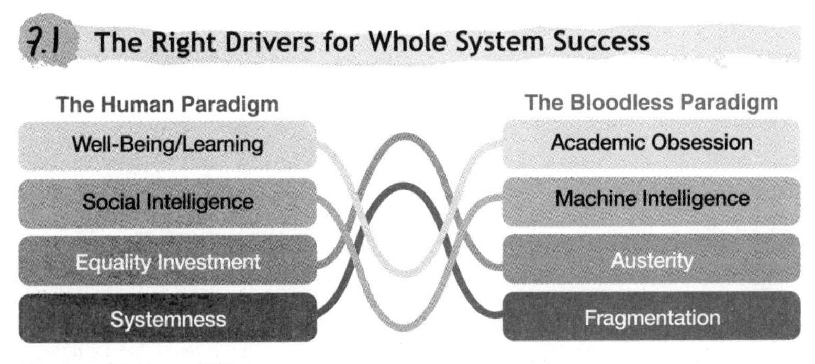

Source: Fullan (2021)

An added problem is that the current system favors the wrong drivers while neglecting the right ones. One additional observation: our eight successful districts managed, against the odds, to leverage the right drivers and dampen the wrong ones. The wrong drivers made the job harder than it should have been, and success less deep than it could have been.

Speaking of depth—over the past six years, Joanne Quinn, Fullan, and the Deep Learning team have developed and implemented with system practitioners in 12 countries a powerful new model compatible with the Hess-Noguera and Shirley-Hargreaves findings and proposals (see Fullan et al., 2018; Quinn et al., 2020; https://deep-learning.global). Our Deep Learning model—which, again, we emphasize, was developed with practitioners—contains four interlocking components. The lead component is *re-setting purpose* (producing students who can "engage the world change the world"). The second consists of the *global competencies (6 Cs)*: character, citizenship, collaboration, communication, creativity, and critical thinking. The third element (and the one missed or underdeveloped by most reformers) is the *four elements of the learning design:* pedagogy, partnerships, learning environment, and digital. The fourth and final component consists of three levels of system culture: *school and community, district/regional,* and *state/policy.* The weakest and most underdeveloped or wrongly developed component is state policy.

CONCLUSION: STUDENTS AS EVOLUTIONARY CHANGEMAKERS

At the end of the day, the most powerful force for societal change is right under our noses: students of all ages. We have not found a student young enough who does not want to be engaged in change. Under current circumstances, the change agent role of students in many cases is dormant. We do not doubt that under the right proactive learning circumstances, the *majority of students* want to become agents of transformation. Is it fair to expect the young to save the world? No, but let's do it anyway.

We believe that there is something mysterious happening in our world at this time. Addressing abject poverty around the globe is foundational to our future—so are new conceptions of learning and who should help lead the transformation. The latter phenomenon has evolutionary properties that concern the relationship between humanity (especially the very young), Mother Nature, and, ultimately, the galaxy. We would need a whole new book to delve deeply into what might be happening, but let's forecast what seems to be the direction. It will come as no surprise to our eight leaders and the thousands of others in their districts that spirit work and the fusion with social relationships in the era in which we live is *transcendental.* It is people's experiences and anxieties that tell us almost daily that this decade is like no other we have encountered.

We venture to say that it is most often the young who intuitively realize that something uncanny and dangerous is happening. We think that the young have a sense that they have a special responsibility to engage differently in learning and in the fate of their individual and collective futures. Indeed, we suggest that young people should be among leading changemakers in society. Our eight districts were not able to go deep or far enough in this direction, but we can speculate about what the next phase might entail.

Learning about and helping to improve the world is the crucial pathway for this decade and beyond. Earlier we mentioned Dennis Shirley and Andy Hargreaves' book, *Five Paths of Student Engagement* (2021); it is surprising to us that these authors do not include "engage the world change the world" as a "path for student engagement." Though they acknowledge that "our world needs a profound transformation . . . and needs to be put back on its axis" (p. 221), Shirley and Hargreaves do not list students as agents of change as one of their five paths. These five paths—intrinsic value, importance, association, empowerment, and mastery—are essential, but we need more.

We agree literally with some of Shirley and Hargreaves' cautions, but young change agents are not literal; they are intuitive, and many are intrinsically interested in learning to go deep with others in a local and worldwide quest. So, we can agree with Shirley and Hargreaves that "automatically associating relevance with engagement can be quite misleading" (p. 82), that the assumption that depth can only be found in "relevant, real-world problems" is mistaken (p. 82), or that "all learning does not have to be immediately relevant" (p. 83). None of these statements that mere relevance is what is required would be embraced by the spirit and collaborative leaders in this book, or by our Deep Learning group (Quinn et al., 2020). These leaders and many students realize that we now live in complex, weird times and that we must do something to address inequality directly, along with other measures to transfigure the systems that govern us.

And that new foundations of learning will be necessary to accomplish this.

We are not asserting that we are exactly right, only that the present—this decade and more—is spiritually different; that many young people sense this; that they want to do something about it; that if cultivated, these numbers will increase; and that our very survival probably depends on large numbers of the young participating as learner-steeped change agents. Thus, *the path to the future must include student engagement as helping to transform the world (and thus the universe).* It is not the *only* learning the young should do, but it must be a core essential feature of the immediate present and beyond.

Let us also acknowledge that this awakening-of-the-young movement is at the very beginning. We don't claim for a moment that it is yet established. For one thing, most of us—young and old—are reeling from the ubiquitous and seemingly relentless pounding of the COVID-19 pandemic and the physical and social calamities coursing through our world. We admit that what we are proposing is spiritual, otherworldly, and unproven. But there is nothing to be lost by embracing this new path, and everything to be gained—as Meg Wheatley reminded us in the foreword, we need "the wisdom of how to be fully human."

As we look to future prospects for radical change, it is interesting and incredibly revealing that Indigenous Nations and Tribal Nations—the young, again—may have a timely sense of what should be pursued in the next stage. It is not that Indigenous communities were right all along (although a case could be made for this), but rather that they too, according to Kahontakwas Diane Longboat, "are reclaiming and revitalizing their cultural traditions and ancestral teachings following colonization." Longboat is a ceremonial leader and member of Turtle Clan and Mohawk Nation at Six Nations in Grand River, Ontario. She describes the recent attention to the powers of some of the very young (birth to age 10, for example) whose gifts are emerging that could bring profound change to bettering the world. Some of the phrases that Longboat uses to capture this emerging Indigenous phenomenon include

> Indigenous knowledge systems; ancient wisdom traditions; spiritual knowledge regarding children passed through the generations; evolution of humanity to understand Spirit, not only cognitive and physical capacities; an evolving consciousness in society in general that strives to connect to another realm of knowing guided by ancestral wisdom; spiritual wisdom of the Ancestors; prophecies of Earth Changes and changes in the Human Being. (personal communication, September 2021)

Recall the observation from evolutionary biologist E. O. Wilson: "Science owns the warrant to explore everything factual . . . but the humanities borne aloft by both past and fantasy have the power of everything . . . conceivable" (2017, p. 70).

Young people of all backgrounds may have more in common about their futures than at any time ever before! Whether this is a bridge too far, or a bridge to nowhere, in one sense doesn't matter. Our conclusion—the conclusion of this book—is that we must enable the very young as deep learning changemakers (it is crucial that they be learners and learned) in relation to the potentially devastating physical and social threats we now face. This is a winning proposal, no matter how you cut it. "Engage the world change the world" integrates learning and transformation. It generates and synchronizes individual and collective growth. Time is running out, but radical breakthroughs may be possible in the next period.

We figure that we have the current decade to get this on the right track. Call it the modern moonshot odyssey. Yes, it is time for society (societies) to help. It is going to require all hands on deck. We all need to learn to live better. The most powerful way to do that is to hitch our future to and with the very young—to help them and to be helped by them *to learn to live to learn!*

REFERENCES

Bentley, T., & Singhania, A. (2020). *Leading through crisis: Resilience, recovery, and renewal.* ACEL Monograph.

Bolman, L., & Deal, T. (2011). *Leading with soul: An uncommon journey of spirit* (3rd ed.). Jossey-Bass.

Boston Consulting Group. (2014). *Teachers know best.* Report Commissioned by the Bill and Melinda Gates Foundation.

Boushey, H. (2019). *Unbound: How inequality constricts our economy and what we can do about it.* Harvard University Press.

Brown, L. (2018). *Culture of love.* WGW Publishing.

Campbell, D., & Fullan, M. (2019). *The governance core.* Corwin.

Campero, A. (2019). *Genes vs cultures vs consciousness: A brief story of our computational minds.* Author.

Christian, B. (2020). *The alignment problem: Machine learning and human values.* W.W. Norton.

Collins, J. (2001). *Good to great.* Harper Collins.

Datnow, A., & Park, V. (2018). *Professional collaboration with purpose.* Routledge.

DePree, M. (2004). *Leadership is an art.* Doubleday.

De Saint-Exupéry, A. (1943). *The little prince.* Alma Books.

Fullan, M. (2008). *The six secrets of change.* Corwin.

Fullan, M. (2010). *All systems go: The change imperative for whole-school reform.* Corwin.

Fullan, M. (2011a). *Choosing the wrong drivers for whole system success.* Centre for Strategic Education.

Fullan, M. (2011b). *The moral imperative realized.* Corwin.

Fullan, M. (2016). *The new meaning of educational change* (5th ed.). Teachers College Press.

Fullan, M. (2019). *Nuance: Why some leaders succeed and others fail.* Corwin.

Fullan, M. (2020a). *Leading in a culture of change* (2nd ed.). Jossey-Bass.

Fullan, M. (2020b). System change in education. *American Journal of Education, 126*, 653–663.

Fullan, M. (2021). *The right drivers for whole system success*. Centre for Strategic Education.

Fullan, M., & Edwards, M. (2017). *The power of unstoppable momentum*. Solution Tree Press.

Fullan, M., & Gallagher, M. J. (2020). *The devil is in the details*. Corwin.

Fullan, M., & Pinchot, M. (2018). The fast track to sustainable turnaround. *Education Leadership, 75*, 48–54.

Fullan, M., & Quinn, J. (2015). *Coherence*. Corwin.

Fullan, M., Quinn, J., & McEachen, J. (2018). *Deep learning: Engage the world change the world*. Corwin.

Fullan, M., Quinn, J., Gardner, M., & Drummy, M. (2020). *Education reimagined: The future of learning*. A collaborative effort between New Pedagogies for Deep Learning (NPDL) and Microsoft Education.

Goodlad, J., & Klein, F. (1970). *Behind the classroom door*. Charles Jones.

Gross, N. C., Giacquinta, J. B. (1971). *Implementing organizational innovation*. Basic Books.

Hargreaves, A. (2019). Teacher collaboration: 30 years of research on its nature, forms, limitations, and effects. *Teachers and Teaching*. https://doi.org/10.1080/13540602.2019.1639499

Hargreaves, A., & Fullan, M. (2012). *Professional capital: Transforming teaching in every school*. Teachers College Press.

Hargreaves, A., & O'Connor, M. (2018). *Collaborative professionalism*. Corwin.

Hattie, J., Fisher, D., Frey, N., & Clarke, S. (2021). *Collective student efficacy*. Corwin.

Hess, F., & Noguera, P. (2021). *A search for common ground*. Teachers College Press.

Isaacson, W. (2014). *The innovators: How a group of hackers, geniuses, and geeks created the digital revolution*. Simon and Schuster.

Kuhn, T. S. (1962). *The structure of scientific revolutions* (4th ed.). University of Chicago Press.

Learning Policy Institute (LPI). (2021). *Chula Vista elementary school district: Positive outliers study*. Author.

Lortie, D. (1975). *School teacher: A sociological study*. University of Chicago Press.

Malin, H. (2018). *Teaching for purpose: Preparing students for lives of meaning*. Harvard Education Press.

Mazzucato, M. (2018). *The value of everything: Making and taking in the global economy*. Hatchette Book Group.

Mazzucato, M. (2021). *Mission economy: A moonshot guide to changing capitalism*. Penguin.

Mehta, J., & Datnow, A. (2020). Changing the grammar of schooling: An appraisal and research agenda. *American Journal of Education*, 126(4), 1–8.

Mehta, J., & Fine, S. (2019). *In search of deep learning*. Harvard University Press.

Organization for Economic Cooperation & Development. (2018). *The teaching and learning international survey (TALIS)*. OECD.

Pinchot, M., & Fullan, M. (2021). *Testing sustainability: How strong school cultures meet disaster*. http://www.ascd.org/ascd-express/vol16/num19/testing-sustainability-how-strong-school-cultures-meet-disaster.aspx

Putnam, R. D., & Garrett, S. R. (2020). *The upswing: How America came together a century ago and how we can do it again*. Simon and Schuster.

Quinn, J., McEachen, J., Fullan, M., Gardner, M., & Drummy, M. (2020). *Dive into deep learning: Tools for engagement*. Corwin.

Robinson, V., Lloyd, C., & Rowe, K. (2008). The impact of leadership on student outcomes. *Education Administration Quarterly, 44*, 635–674.

Sarason, S. (1972). *The culture of the school and the problem of change*. Allyn & Bacon.

Shirley, D., & Hargreaves, A. (2021). *Five paths of student engagement*. Solution Tree Press.

Singhania, A., Hard, N., & Bentley, T. (2020). *Unleashing the power of the collective in education*. RMIT University, Social Ventures Australia (SVA).

Testino, L. (2021, April 16). SCS "reimagine" plan proposes new district name, school buildings, higher teacher pay. *The Commercial Appeal*. https://www.commercialappeal.com/story/news/education/2021/04/16/watch-live-shelby-county-schools-delivers-first-state-district-since-pandemic/7243877002/

Wallace-Wells, D. (2019). *The uninhabitable earth: Life after warming*. Tim Duggan Books.

Wheatley, M. (2009). *Turning to one another: Simple conversations to restore hope to the future*. Berrett-Koehler.

Wheatley, M., & Kellner-Rogers, M. (1966, 1999). *A simpler way*. Berrett-Koehler.

Wilson, D. S. (2019). *This view of life*. Pantheon.

Wilson, E. O. (2014). *The meaning of human existence*. W. W. Norton.

Wilson, E. O (2017). *The origins of creativity*. W. W. Norton.

INDEX

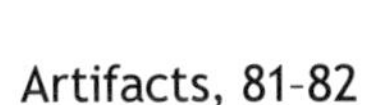

ACKNOWLEDGMENTS

Our overwhelming thanks to the eight superintendents who gave unstintingly of their time to us, and for their magnificent contributions to spirit work and the science of collaboration. To Meg Wheatley for her spontaneous and enthusiastic commitment to writing a brilliant and deep foreword. Thanks to Claudia Cuttress who took charge of the manuscript—no one combines quality, speed, and creativity like Claudia does. To Autumn Hampton for the inspiring and beautiful cover design. And to Corwin, especially Ariel Curry and Melanie Birdsall, who provided great advice and support at all stages of production and produced the book on a very short timeline.

—Michael and Mark

To thank everyone I should by name would fill several pages. I have to be brief. I owe great thanks to our Deep Learning team, storming the world with great spirit and partnership. To the Stuart Foundation for supporting our system work in California. To system colleagues for getting ever so close to improving whole systems of learning. To my family, what can I say? Wife Wendy is a loving, imaginative, and full-on stalwart in my life. My five children—to be so close after all these years is a blessing. I am proud and lucky. Finally, to Mark, who himself is a remarkable and inspirational spirit leader—how could two so different people make such a smooth and productive team? Thanks all!

—Michael

A special thank you to every teacher, principal, administrator, custodian, bus driver, food service staff, and clerical staff for your dedication and spirit work. To my wife Marcia, and family

Luke, Autumn, Jared, Adrian, and Harlan, thanks for your constant nurturance. Thank you, Michael, for years of leadership and service for students around the world and for the honor of working with you.

—Mark

ABOUT THE AUTHORS

Michael Fullan, Order of Canada, is the former Dean and Professor Emeritus of the Ontario Institute for Studies in Education/University of Toronto. He is co-leader of New Pedagogies for Deep Learning (NPDL) and a worldwide authority on educational change and system transformation. Fullan is a prolific award-winning author whose books have been published in several languages. He holds five honorary doctorates from universities around the world. His latest books are *Nuance, Deep Learning: Engage the World Change the World* (with Joanne Quinn and Joanne McEachen), and *The Devil Is in the Details* (with Mary Jean Gallagher).

Mark Edwards previously served as school superintendent in Danville, Virginia, and in Henrico County, Virginia, where he was named the Virginia Superintendent of the Year in 2001 and received the Harold McGraw Prize in Education in 2003. He later served as superintendent of the Mooresville Graded School District in North Carolina. Edwards was named the North Carolina Superintendent of the Year as well as the AASA National Superintendent of the Year in 2013. He received North Carolina's prestigious Order of the Long Leaf Pine Award in 2013 and the Public School Forum of North Carolina Jay Robinson Education Leadership Award in 2014. He has been recognized as a pioneer in one-to-one computing and as a collaborative leader in public education. Edwards has published three books, *Every Child Every Day: A Digital Conversion Model for Student Achievement*, *Thank You for Your Leadership: The Power of Distributed Leadership in a Digital Conversion Model*, and co-authored *The Power of Unstoppable Momentum* with Michael Fullan.

Also Available

SIMON BREAKSPEAR & BRONWYN RYRIE JONES

Realistic in demand and innovative in approach, this practical and powerful improvement process is designed to help all teachers get going, and keep going, with incremental professional improvement in schools.

JAMES BAILEY & RANDY WEINER

The thought-provoking daily reflections in this guided journal are designed to strengthen the social and emotional skills of leaders and create a strong social-emotional environment for leaders, teachers, and students.

MARK WHITE & DWIGHT L. CARTER

Through understanding the past and envisioning the future, the authors use practical exercises and real-life examples to draw the blueprint for adapting schools to the age of hyper-change.

ALLAN G. OSBORNE, JR. & CHARLES J. RUSSO

With its user-friendly format, this resource will help educators understand the law so they can focus on providing exemplary education to students.

MICHAEL FULLAN & MARY JEAN GALLAGHER

With the goal of transforming the culture of learning to develop greater equity, excellence, and student well-being, this book will help you liberate the system and maintain focus.

TOM VANDER ARK & EMILY LIEBTAG

Diverse case studies and a framework based on timely issues help educators focus students' talents and interests on developing an entrepreneurial mindset and leadership skills.

THOMAS HATCH

By highlighting what works and demonstrating what can be accomplished if we redefine conventional schools, we can have more efficient, more effective, and more equitable schools and create powerful opportunities to support all aspects of students' development.

LYN SHARRATT

Explore 14 essential parameters to guide system and school leaders toward building powerful collaborative learning cultures.

CORWIN